Yilin
Illustrated
Classics

有声双语经典

Comedies from Shakespeare
莎士比亚喜剧故事

［英国］威廉·莎士比亚 著
［英国］伊迪丝·内斯比特 改写
黄晓丽 译

译林出版社

微信扫描二维码收听英文有声书

每一个灯光漫溢的夜晚

去年开始，京东图书商城的运营者们在网上做了一档很不错的栏目，叫作"大咖书单"，我记得是在第四期时，我为这份书单推荐了两本书，《杀死一只知更鸟》和《奇风岁月》，到第七期又推荐了两本，《老师，水缸破了!》和《天虹战队小学》。回过头一想，赫然惊觉，两次推荐的四本书，居然都是出自译林出版社。潜意识里我对这家出版社是有多偏爱啊，我那么自觉自愿地、一往无前地做了译林社的一名"吹鼓手"。

没有办法，喜欢就是喜欢，没有道理可讲。

喜欢译林出版社的书，其实是因为我喜欢外国文学作品。细究起来，我对外国文学的热爱，源自童年那个无书可读的时代。我在扬子江边一个小小的县城长大，我父母工作的学校是当地最好的县中，县中图书馆多少有一些藏书，"文革"开始的那一年，书籍和老师们一同被揪出来示众，之后老师们游街，图书拉到操场一把火烧毁。图书馆主任"火中抢栗"，偷出一纸箱运回家中。主任的儿子跟我小学同班，因此我沾了他的光，把他父亲秘藏的小说书一本一本地搬运出来，在一双双黝黑的小手中辗转一圈之后，再神不知鬼不觉地偷放回去。那位图书馆主任可能比较"崇洋媚外"，弄回家的小说大都是世界名著，我对于外国文学的兴趣，便是从那时开始的。

那时年幼，读书不求甚解，又因为是背着大人们的"偷阅"，读书过程基本是囫囵吞枣。很多书传到我手里的时候缺头少尾，只剩下中间三分之二的篇幅，精彩之处戛然而止，急得我抓耳挠腮。页码齐全的书，抓到手里翻开就读，书名是什么，作者何人，很奇怪地忽略不计，一点儿不想知道。及至十年之后我上了大学，外国文学开禁，我在北大图书馆发疯一样地狂读名著时，时不时会在心里惊叫一声：这本书不是我小时候读过的吗？于是，嗅着书中陈年纸张散发的潮湿气味，心里涌出一种老朋友失而复得的狂喜。也有一些书，童年时候莫名其妙地读过了，却是踏破铁鞋无觅处。它们就这样永远地从我的生活中消失了，像无数消失在我生命旅途的朋友和家人。

高二那年，妹妹的同学借了我一套肖洛霍夫的《静静的顿河》。在我的生命中，那是一次飞跃，此后的这么多年我以文学为生，应该与那一次的阅读震撼有关。书中的那个哥萨克人格利高里，很长时间中成为我欣赏男性的标准。书中描写的顿河风光，至今都在我的脑子里鲜活和闪亮。

　　十九岁，我在农场插队。一个飘雪的冬夜，农场宣传队在场部排练节目时，电突然停了，礼堂里一片漆黑。一个只读了三年小学的农场工人对我们说："我来讲个故事吧。"他讲的那个故事叫《茶花女》。一直到今天我都觉得那个晚上的情景像梦。在那个不准读书的年代，那个没有文化的乡村，初小没有毕业的农民居然讲出法国作家小仲马的名著。那个漆黑凄美的冬夜，从此也深深刻印到我的记忆之中。那是我第一次领略悲剧作品的魅力。几年之后，时代剧变，我买到了《茶花女》的小说，听过了《茶花女》的歌剧，看过了同名电影，我从一切形式的《茶花女》中寻找那个雪夜的感觉，然而再不可能，最好的都是唯一的。

　　一九七八年初春进入北大，那一年外国文学还没有开禁，北大图书馆里辟出很小的一个房间作为"外国文学阅览室"，每星期三的下午，允许中文系文学专业的学生，凭学生证进入阅读。我的印象中，那间阅览室只能容纳十几二十几个学生，每次开放，排在前面的同学才有机会被老师放进门去。于是那一年的"星期三"成了我们的排队日，匆忙吃过午饭，碗都来不及洗，拔脚往图书馆飞奔，一行人安静地在阅览室门外排队，等待两点钟开门放人。除却寒暑假、节日、有课的日子、有重要活动的日子，剩下的"星期三"并不是很多，所以每一次的阅读时间弥足珍贵。一书在手，全身心地扑上去吞食，每每到五点钟闭馆交书，站起身来，头晕目眩，虚脱的感觉。那种阅读，耗出去的不仅仅是脑力，还有巨大的体力。

一九七八年，人民文学出版社开始重印外国文学名著。刚开始的时候人多书少，全班同学轮流着到海淀新华书店通宵排队购书。那时年轻，通宵不眠为了买一本书，丝毫不觉辛苦。慢慢地书越出越多，时常到书店转悠，冷不丁地就碰上新书上架。排长队是不必了，痛切的感觉是口袋里钱太少。那时发下的心愿是哪一天发了财，可以把书店里的新书都掳回来。转眼三十年过去，谈不上发大财，买书是可以不计价钱了，可是看着书店里铺天盖地的图书，想到书架上还有很多书不及阅读，解囊的兴致少了许多，挑挑拣拣，带个一两本回家，心中并没有太多欣喜。人生的悲哀真正是无处不在。

还是回到一九七九年。印象之中，《世界文学》《外国文艺》《译林》这些杂志都是在那时候陆续复刊和创刊的。这些刊物着重介绍外国现当代文学，并且以中短篇幅的为主，对于习惯了阅读古典长篇的我们，眼前似乎又打开了另外一个世界。我非常清楚地记得，同班同学陈建功有一次读到格雷厄姆·格林的短篇《永远占有》，佩服得五体投地，双眼发光地跑来跟我们说："我真想跪在格林面前向他致敬！"

童年的阅读实在重要，它奠定了一个人终生的阅读口味。检点我书架上的书籍，百分之八十是外国文学作品。我曾经订阅过的刊物，有《世界文学》《外国文艺》《译林》《译文》《世界电影》……统统跟外国文学有关。几十年中，每一个灯光漫溢的夜晚，阅读这些缤纷华彩的文字，感觉世界离我很近。文字中写到的每一个角落，都是我心灵去过的地方。我占有了这些作品，我就占有了这个世界。

在我的印象中，译林社出的每一本书，无论是社科类的，还是人文类的，都值得读者收藏。而在译林社所出的文学类图书中，外国儿童文学作品又属精品中的精品，比之国内大多数专业少儿社所出的图书，译林社的视野更宽，选择标准更高，口味也更纯粹。很敬佩译林社的众多编辑，他们敬业而又专业，总是能从全世界浩如烟海的各类书籍中挑选出最值得国人阅读的那一部分，延请最好的翻译家、最好的画家和设计师，做出一本又一本端庄而精致的图书，送到读者的面前。每次徜徉在灯光明亮的书店，或者打开手机上网搜索，译林社的新书总是我最中意的目标，我信赖译林社的出品，而且基本上不会失望。

翻开这套"有声双语经典"的书目，里面的作家和作品都是我熟悉的名字。有些书是在童年和少年时代各种侥幸落入我的手中的，有些是读大学时列入必读书单需要细读的，还有一些，比如《小王子》，比如《绿山墙的安妮》，少年和青年时代居然都错失了它们，是我在人到中年之后才补读完成。更有一部分，年轻时读过，花甲之年又重新捧起，是为了重温之后可以为我的小外孙女们详细讲解。在此我愿意把这些书目推荐给小读者们，是因为这样的一套书当之无愧地应该成为你们最好的朋友，会帮助你们更加优雅地长大。

黄蓓佳

作品导读

　　莎士比亚的喜剧成就与其悲剧一样卓著。除《仲夏夜之梦》《威尼斯商人》《第十二夜》《皆大欢喜》这脍炙人口的"四大喜剧"外，《无事生非》《暴风雨》《冬天的故事》《终成眷属》等名作也是影响至今的喜剧典范。

　　这些剧作大都以爱情、友谊为主题，蕴含着人文主义的美好理想，洋溢着乐观主义的情调。在莎翁设置的巧妙情节中，主人公热爱生活、追求自由与幸福，他们以智慧与美德为乐，同自私、伪善、贪婪等人性之恶做斗争，向衰朽、封建的社会发起挑战。

　　其中的剧情为后世作家提供了无尽的创作灵感。比如，《傲慢与偏见》中达西与伊丽莎白这对欢喜冤家，是不是同《无事生非》中贝特丽丝与培尼狄克这一相爱相杀的组合特别相似？莎剧中的许多人物深入人心，比如《威尼斯商人》

中的夏洛克早已成了"吝啬"的同义词。难能可贵的是，早在文艺复兴时期，莎翁就刻画出了鲜明的女性形象，她们坚定、智慧、勇敢，充满了蓬勃的生命力。

在《威尼斯商人》中，鲍西娅集美貌、财富、智慧于一身，面对众多慕名而来的追求者，她不看重财富地位，而是将人品作为衡量标准，她聪明地设置小游戏，从而选出了真诚的巴萨尼奥。在丈夫的朋友安东尼奥陷入险境时，她女扮男装成律师，在法庭上凭借胆识与机智，既维护了法律的尊严，又惩治了用心险恶的放贷人夏洛克。

在《第十二夜》中，薇奥拉遭遇海难，与双胞胎哥哥失散，独自流落到伊利里亚。她乔装改扮，用哥哥西巴斯辛的身份做了奥西诺公爵的仆人，代公爵向心上人奥丽维娅求爱。虽然薇奥拉深爱公爵，却将爱埋于心底，兢兢业业地履行着职责。幸好西巴斯辛及时出现，与奥丽维娅相爱，薇奥拉终于可以勇敢地表明女儿身，也表达对公爵的爱意。她以自己敏捷的头脑、忠诚的责任感赢得了公爵的心。

在《终成眷属》中，海伦娜爱上了英俊但浪荡的伯爵贝特兰，可是贝特兰看不起出身低微的海伦娜。海伦娜并不气馁，她以高超的医术治好了国王的病，赢得了国王的赐婚。她机智而坚定，施展巧计得到了贝特兰的爱情信物——祖传的戒指，最终不仅俘获了贝特兰的心，也使堕落的伯爵受到教训，愿意做一个正直的人。

四百多年过去了，社会观念有了巨大的进步，但这些女性形象依然熠熠生辉，具有积极的意义。莎剧至今仍是戏剧史上难以企及的高峰，也滋养着一代代读者的心灵。歌德曾说："我读到他的第一页，我的一生就从此属于他了。"是的，与莎剧相遇的那一刻，我们便开启了一段美好的旅程，它的魅力将吸引我们不断探索，加深对文本、对世界，还有对我们自身的认识。

（黄晓丽／文）

作家简介

威廉·莎士比亚（William Shakespeare, 1564—1616），华人世界尊称为莎翁，是英国文学史上最杰出的作家之一。莎士比亚戏剧被译为多种主要语言，表演次数远远超过其他任何戏剧家的作品，对后世的戏剧和文学产生了深刻而持久的影响。

莎士比亚 1564 年 4 月 23 日出生于英国沃里克郡埃文河畔的斯特拉福，父亲约翰·莎士比亚是一位殷实的手套商人和市参议员。十八岁时，他与安妮·海瑟薇结婚，共生育了三名子女。16 世纪末到 17 世纪初，莎士比亚离开家乡，在伦敦开始演员生涯，并尝试创作剧本。

1590 年到 1613 年是莎士比亚创作的黄金时期。他早期主要写喜剧与历史剧，风格明朗乐观，著名的四大喜剧《威尼斯商人》《仲夏夜之梦》《皆大欢喜》《第十二夜》

便写于 16 世纪的最后十年。1600 年到 1608 年是创作的中期，达到其成就的巅峰，主要写悲剧，揭露社会的种种罪恶和黑暗，描写牺牲与复仇，风格阴郁悲愤，这一时期创作的四大悲剧《奥瑟罗》《哈姆莱特》《李尔王》《麦克白》是公认的英语最佳范例。在人生的最后阶段，莎士比亚主要创作悲喜剧，又称传奇剧，风格浪漫空幻，比如《辛白林》等。

1613 年前后，莎士比亚退休，离开伦敦，回到埃文河畔的斯特拉福。1616 年，他在故乡去世，安葬于当地的圣三一教堂。

从 1594 年开始，莎士比亚的一些剧本以四开本出版。1623 年，他生前所在剧团的两位同事出版了"第一对开本"，除《两位贵族亲戚》和《泰尔亲王佩力克尔斯》外，目前已被认可的莎士比亚剧作均收录其中。"第一对开本"很多地方根据记忆重新写成，并且在"四开本"与"第一对开本"之间，莎士比亚做过多处修订，因此同一剧本会有多个版本传世。

身后二百年，莎士比亚声誉日隆，他的剧作逐渐成为世界文学不可逾越的巅峰之一，也在后世文学巨擘的作品中留下了不可磨灭的印痕。他影响了哈代、福克纳、狄更斯、梅尔维尔等众多一流小说家。他对很多画家也有潜移默化的影响，甚至精神分析学家弗洛伊德在他的人性理论中也分析了莎剧中的人物，比如哈姆莱特的心理。

1902 年，梁启超率先将"Shakespeare"译为"莎士比亚"，此后一百余年，林纾、田汉、梁实秋、俞步凡等名家都译介过莎翁作品。朱生豪先生从 1935 年开始，到 1944 年病逝为止，译出了三十一部半莎剧，译文质量、风格上乘，获得国内外莎士比亚研究者的认可。

（黄晓丽 / 文）

目 录

仲夏夜之梦

❧

　　赫米娅和拉山德是一对恋人，但是赫米娅的父亲希望她嫁给一个叫狄米特律斯的男子。

　　在他们居住的雅典，有一部糟糕的法律，规定任何拒绝按照父亲的意愿结婚的女孩，都可以被处死。赫米娅的父亲因为赫米娅拒绝按他的意愿行事而非常生气，于是把她带到雅典公爵面前，要求如果她仍然拒绝服从他的命令，就处死她。公爵给她四天时间考虑这个问题，如果继续拒绝嫁给狄米特律斯，她就得死。

　　当然，拉山德伤心得快要疯了，他认为最好的办法就是赫米娅逃到他姑母家，那里不受那严酷法律的约束。他会去那里找赫米娅并娶她为妻。但在动身之前，赫米娅告诉了朋友海伦娜她要做什么。

A MIDSUMMER-NIGHT'S DREAM.

早在狄米特律斯和赫米娅谈婚论嫁之前，海伦娜就已经爱上狄米特律斯了。她很傻，像所有被嫉妒蒙蔽了眼睛的人一样，她看不出狄米特律斯希望迎娶赫米娅而不是他的爱恋者海伦娜一事并不能怪可怜的赫米娅。她知道，如果她告诉狄米特律斯赫米娅要到雅典城外的树林去，狄米特律斯就会跟着赫米娅。她心里想："这样我就可以跟着他，至少我可以看到他。"于是她找到狄米特律斯，泄露了朋友的秘密。

　　拉山德要去同赫米娅会合的这片树林，也是另外两个人决定跟随他们去的地方，和大多数树林一样，里面到处都是仙子。这天晚上，仙王奥布朗和仙后提泰妮娅就在这片树林里。仙子是非常聪明的，但有时他们也会像人类一样愚蠢。奥布朗和提泰妮娅本可以再幸福不过，却在一场愚蠢的争吵中把快乐全都抛弃了。他们一见面就说不愉快的话，互相咒骂，以至于所有的仙子随从都害怕得爬进橡实壳里藏起来。

　　于是，仙王和他的侍从在树林的一边活动，仙后和她的侍从则在另一边活动；而不是一起在月光下彻夜跳舞，让宫廷随时充满欢声笑语。引起这一切麻烦的是一个印度小男孩，提泰妮娅安排男孩做她的侍童。奥布朗想要这个男孩跟着他，成为他的一名骑士，但仙后不肯把男孩交出去。

这一天晚上，在月光下长满青苔的林间空地上，仙王和仙后相遇了。

"真不巧在月光下遇见你，骄傲的提泰妮娅。"仙王说。

"什么？善妒的奥布朗！"仙后回答，"你的争吵毁了一切。走吧，仙子们，我们离他远远的。我现在不想和他做朋友了。"

"是你引起争吵的。"仙王说。

"把那个印度男孩给我吧，我将再次成为你卑微的仆人和追求者。"

"请死心吧，"仙后说，"用你的整个仙国都不能从我这换到那个男孩。走吧，仙子们。"

她和她的侍从们在月光下离去。

"好，去你的吧，"奥布朗说，"但在你离开这片林子之前，我一定会和你算账的。"

然后，奥布朗叫来他最喜欢的小仙迫克。迫克是个淘气鬼。他常常溜进奶牛场，拿走奶油，钻进搅拌机，这样就产不出黄油来；他让啤酒变酸；在漆黑的夜晚，他引人们误入迷途，再嘲笑他们；当人们要坐下时，他把凳子从他们屁股底下抽走让他们摔坐在地上；当人们要喝热麦芽酒时，他把酒打翻在他们的下巴上。

"现在，"奥布朗对这个小仙说，"把那朵'爱懒花'给我摘来。如果把那紫色小花的汁液滴在睡梦中人的眼皮上，他们便会爱上醒来看见的第一样生物。我要把这种花的汁液滴在我的提泰妮娅的眼皮上，等她醒来，她看到的第一样东西，无论是狮子、熊、狼、公牛也好，或是好事的猴子、忙碌的猿猴也好，她都会爱上的。"

迫克走后，狄米特律斯穿过林间空地，可怜的海伦娜跟在他身后。海伦娜还在告诉狄米特律斯她是多么爱他，并提醒狄米特律斯许下的所有诺言，而狄米特律斯仍然告诉她，他从不爱她也不可能爱她，他的诺言什么也不是。奥布朗为可怜的海伦娜难过，当迫克带着花回来时，他命令迫克跟着狄米特律斯，并在他的眼皮上滴一些花汁，这样当他醒来看到海伦娜时，就会像海伦娜爱他一样爱海伦娜。于是，迫克出发了，他在树林里游逛，但他找到的不是狄米特律斯，而是拉山德，他把花汁滴在了拉山德的眼皮上。但拉山德醒来时看到的不是他的赫米娅，而是正在树林中寻找狠心的狄米特律斯的海伦娜。他一见到海伦娜就爱上了她，在紫色小花的魔力下，他离开了自己的爱人。

赫米娅醒来后发现拉山德不见了，她在树林里四处寻找。迫克回去告诉了奥布朗他所做的一切，奥布朗很快就发现他弄错了，于是开始寻找狄米特律斯。他找到狄米特律斯后，就把花的汁液滴在他眼皮上。狄米特律斯醒来后看到的第一样生物也是海伦娜。狄米特律斯和拉山德都跟着她穿过树林，现在轮到赫米娅像海伦娜从前一样跟着她的情人了。海伦娜和赫米娅开始争吵，狄米特律斯和拉山德也打起来。奥布朗本想帮助这两对恋人，结果好心办坏事，他非常难过。他对迫克说：

"这两个年轻人要打起来了。你必须用浓雾遮住夜空，引他们迷路，不要让他们碰到一起。等他们累坏了，就会睡着。再把另一种草汁滴在拉山德的眼皮上。这能让他恢复从前的眼光和爱情。这样，每个男人都会得到爱他的女人，他们都会认为这只是一场仲夏夜之梦。等这事办完，就万事大吉了。"

于是，迫克就照他说的去做，等他们两人没有见面就睡着了，迫克把汁液滴到拉山德的眼皮上，说：

> 当你醒来时，
>
> 会得到真正的快乐，
>
> 当看到曾经的爱人的眼睛，
>
> 哥儿爱着姐儿，
>
> 一切都将正常。

与此同时，奥布朗找到睡在河岸上的提泰妮娅，那里开满了各种花。提泰妮娅夜里经常裹着蛇皮睡在那里。奥布朗弯下身子，把汁液滴在她的眼皮上，说：

为你醒来时所看到的，

付出你的真爱。

　　当提泰妮娅醒来时，她看到的第一样东西是一个愚蠢的小丑，那是一群到树林里排练的伶人中的一个。这个小丑遇到了迫克，迫克把一个驴脑袋套在他的头上，看起来就像长在那里一样。提泰妮娅一觉醒来，看到这头可怕的怪物，她说："这是什么天使？你既聪明又美丽吧？"

　　"如果我足够聪明，能找到走出这片树林的路，那就够了。"愚蠢的小丑说。

　　"别想走出树林。"提泰妮娅说。花汁的魔力在她身上生效，在她看来，小丑是世界上最美丽、最可爱的生物。"我爱你，"她继续说，"跟我来，我会派仙子侍候你。"

　　随后，她叫来四个仙子，他们的名字分别是豆花、蛛网、飞蛾和芥子。

　　"你们必须侍候好这位先生，"仙后说，"给他吃杏子、露莓、紫葡萄、绿无花果和桑葚。把熊蜂的蜜囊偷来，取下彩蝶的翅膀，扇去他睡眼中的月光。"

　　"遵命。"其中一个仙子说。其他仙子都说："遵命。"

　　"现在，和我一起坐下，"仙后对小丑说，"让我摸摸你可爱的脸颊，我要把麝香玫瑰插在你光滑的脑袋上，我要吻你美丽的大耳朵，我温柔的宝贝儿。"

"豆花在哪里?"戴着驴头的小丑问道。他不太在意仙后的爱情,但有仙子侍候他,他感到非常自豪。"在这里。"豆花说。

"替我挠挠头,豆花。"小丑说,"蛛网在哪里?""在这里。"蛛网说。

小丑说:"替我杀死那边蓟草叶尖上的熊蜂,把它的蜜囊拿来。芥子在哪里?""在这里。"芥子说。

"哦,我什么也不想要,"小丑说,"只是想让你帮蛛网给我挠挠痒。我想我得去理发了,因为我觉得我的脸毛茸茸的。"

"你想吃点什么?"仙后说。

"我想要一些干燕麦,"小丑说,因为他的驴脑袋让他想吃驴的食物,"还有一些干草。"

"要不要我的仙子去松鼠洞里给你拿些新鲜坚果来?"仙后问。

"我宁愿吃一两把上好的干豌豆,"小丑说,"但请不要让你的人打扰我;我要睡觉了。"

听了这话,仙后说:"让我把你抱在怀里。"

于是,当奥布朗来到的时候,他发现他美丽的仙后正在亲吻一个戴着驴头的小丑。在把仙后从魔法中解救出来之前,他说服仙后把他梦寐以求的印度男孩给了他。然后,他怜悯起仙后来,在她美丽的眼睛上滴了一点祛除魔法的花汁。片刻之后，她便看清了她曾那么喜爱的驴头小丑，知道自己是多么愚蠢。奥布朗把驴头从小丑颈上取下来，让他的蠢脑袋枕在花上睡个好觉。

这样，一切都恢复如常了。奥布朗和提泰妮娅比以前更相爱了。狄米特律斯只爱海伦娜，而海伦娜则除了狄米特律斯之外从来没有爱过任何人。至于赫米娅和拉山德，他们是你能遇到的最恩爱的一对，即使仙林中也无人能出其右。

于是，这两对凡人回到雅典并结婚了；而仙王和仙后直到今天仍然恩爱地住在那片树林里。

威尼斯商人

安东尼奥是威尼斯富有的商人。他的船几乎遍布各个海域，他与葡萄牙、墨西哥、英格兰和印度都有贸易往来。虽然他为自己的财富骄傲，但他十分慷慨，乐于用这些钱来帮助朋友，在这些朋友中，巴萨尼奥位列第一。

现在，巴萨尼奥和其他许多快活又勇敢的绅士一样，鲁莽而奢侈，他发现自己不仅把财产花光了，而且无力偿还欠债，只能向安东尼奥求助。

"安东尼奥，"他说，"我欠你的钱和感情最多。我已经想好了一个计划，只要你愿意帮助我，我就可以还清我所欠的一切。"

"你说说我能做什么，我就去做。"他的朋友回答。

巴萨尼奥说："贝尔蒙特有一位富有的小姐，向她求

THE MERCHANT of VENICE

13

婚的人来自世界各地，他们都名声显赫，因为这位女士不仅富有，而且美丽善良。上次我们见面的时候，她对我的态度是那么好，我相信只要我有办法去她居住的贝尔蒙特，就能打败所有对手，赢得她的爱。"

"我所有的财产，"安东尼奥说，"都在海上，所以我没有现钱；幸运的是，我在威尼斯信誉很好，我愿意为你去借你需要的钱。"

当时，威尼斯住着一位富有的放债人，名叫夏洛克。安东尼奥非常鄙视厌恶这个人，以最严厉和最轻蔑的态度对待他。他把夏洛克拒之门外，甚至朝夏洛克吐口水。夏洛克忍下所有这些侮辱，只是耐心地耸耸肩；但在内心深处，他十分渴望报复这名富有的、自以为是的商人。"我就是要比安东尼奥还多拥有五十万金币。在市场上，他无论到哪里，都谴责我收取高利息，更糟糕的是，他借钱给别人不收一分钱利息。"

巴萨尼奥找到夏洛克，请他借给安东尼奥三千金币，为期三个月；夏洛克隐藏了内心的仇恨，对安东尼奥说："尽管你对我十分粗暴，我还是愿意和你做朋友，赢得你的爱。所以我会借钱给你，而且不收取任何利息。不过，只是为了好玩，你得立下一份借据，约定如果你三个月后不还我钱，我就有权从你身上割一磅肉，我想割你身上哪个部位的肉，就割哪个部位的肉。"

“不，”巴萨尼奥对他的朋友叫道，“你不要为我冒这样的风险。”

“怎么，别担心，”安东尼奥说，“我的船会在借款到期前一个月回来。我来签借据。”

这样，巴萨尼奥就可以去贝尔蒙特，在那里向美丽的鲍西娅求爱。就在他动身的那天晚上，放债人的漂亮女儿杰西卡从家里逃走，和她的情人私奔了，她从父亲的宝库里拿走了几袋金币和宝石。夏洛克的悲伤和愤怒令人害怕。他对杰西卡的爱变成了恨。“我宁愿她死在我的脚下，那些珠宝还戴在她的耳朵上。”他叫道。现在，他唯一的安慰是听说安东尼奥遭受严重的损失，其中有几艘船失事。“让他兑现他的借据，”夏洛克说，“让他兑现他的借据。”

与此同时，巴萨尼奥到达贝尔蒙特，拜访了美丽的鲍西娅。他发现，正如他告诉安东尼奥的那样，关于鲍西娅的财富和美貌的传闻吸引了来自四面八方的求婚者。但是鲍西娅对他们都只有一个回答。她只接受保证会遵守她父亲遗嘱的求婚者。这个条件吓跑了许多热情的追求者。因为谁想赢得鲍西娅的心，就得猜出三只匣子里的哪一只装着她的肖像。如果他猜对了，鲍西娅就会成为他的新娘；如果他没猜对，他就必须履行誓约，永远不透露他选择了哪只匣子，永远不结婚，并且马上离开此地。

三只匣子分别用金、银、铅铸成。金匣子上写着这样的题词："谁选择我，将得到众人之所愿。"银匣子上这样写道："谁选择我，将得到他所应得的。"铅匣子上是如下内容："谁选择我，必须冒失去一切的风险。"摩洛哥亲王，作为一个勇敢的黑人，是最先接受考验的人之一。他选择了金匣子，他说银匣子和铅匣子都装不下鲍西娅的肖像。他在里面发现一张字条，上面写着众人之所愿——死亡。

在他之后，骄傲的阿拉贡亲王说："让我拥有我所应得的——我当然应该得到这位小姐。"他选择了银匣子，里面的字条上画了一个傻瓜的头。"我只应该得到一个傻瓜的头吗？"他叫道。

最后，巴萨尼奥来了，鲍西娅担心他选错，想阻止他做出选择。因为她深爱着巴萨尼奥，就像巴萨尼奥爱她一样。"但是，"巴萨尼奥说，"让我马上选择吧，因为我现在像在刑架上受刑一样。"

随后，鲍西娅吩咐仆人们在她勇敢的恋人做选择时奏响音乐。在乐师轻轻演奏时，巴萨尼奥起了誓，然后走向匣子。"仅仅外表所呈现的，"他说，"不见得是真相。世人容易被表面的虚饰所欺蒙，所以我既不选金的也不选银的，我选铅的。但愿结果是好的！"他打开铅匣子，发现里面装有美丽的鲍西娅的肖像，他转向鲍西娅，询问她是不是真的属于他了。

"是的，"鲍西娅说，"我是你的了，这座房子也是你的了，我把这枚戒指送给你，你永远不能把它弄丢。"

巴萨尼奥说他高兴得几乎说不出话来，他发誓只要他活着，就决不会把这枚戒指弄丢。

突然，他所有的幸福被悲哀摧毁，原来从威尼斯来的信使告诉他，安东尼奥破产了，夏洛克请公爵要求安东尼奥履行约定，根据借据，他有权得到商人安东尼奥的一磅肉。鲍西娅听说巴萨尼奥的朋友有危险，也像巴萨尼奥一样伤心。

"首先，"她说，"和我到教堂结成夫妇，然后立刻去威尼斯帮助你的朋友。你要带上比借款多二十倍的钱去还债。"

新婚丈夫走后，鲍西娅紧随其后，化装成律师来到威尼斯，她带来了著名律师培拉里奥的介绍信，原来威尼斯公爵请培拉里奥来判决夏洛克为得到安东尼奥的一磅肉，所提起的诉讼。在法庭上，巴萨尼奥提出给夏洛克两倍的钱，只要他能撤回起诉。但是放债人的唯一回答是：

即使你那六千金币的每一块都分成六份，

每一份都是一块金币，

我也不会接受它们，我只要履行约定。

就在这时，乔装的鲍西娅来了，连她的丈夫也没有认出她来。她带来了赫赫有名的培拉里奥的介绍信，因此公爵欢迎她，并让她来处理这件事。随后，她用高贵的话语请求夏洛克仁慈一点。但是夏洛克对她的请求充耳不闻。

"我就要得到那一磅肉。"他回答。

"你有什么话要说吗？"鲍西娅问商人。

"没什么话，"他回答说，"我已准备好了。"

"法庭判给你一磅安东尼奥的肉。"鲍西娅对放债人说。

"最公正的法官！"夏洛克叫道，"判决来了：来，准备好。"

"等一下。这份借据只说你可以割安东尼奥的肉，没说你可以流他的血。如果你让他流了一滴血，你的财产就会被没收，归国家所有。法律就是这样规定的。"

夏洛克害怕地说："那我就接受巴萨尼奥的提议吧。"

"不，"鲍西娅严厉地说，"除了借据上写的，你什么都不能要。取走你那一磅肉，但请记住，无论你割多了还是割少了，即使相差一根头发的重量，你都会失去财产和生命。"

夏洛克现在非常害怕。"把我借给他的三千金币还给我，放他走。"

巴萨尼奥本来打算还钱给他，但鲍西娅说："不！除了借据上写的，什么都不能给他。"

"你，一个外邦人，"她补充说，"试图夺走一名威尼斯公民的性命，根据威尼斯法律，你的性命和财产都将被剥夺。跪下来，请求公爵开恩吧。"

就这样，形势发生了逆转，要不是安东尼奥说情，夏洛克就不会得到从宽发落。事实上，放债人一半的财产收归国家，而另一半财产他必须赠给他的女婿，但即便如此他也心满意足了。

巴萨尼奥为了感谢聪明的律师，在诱导之下把妻子给他的戒指送给了别人，而他曾经承诺和那枚戒指永不分离。回到贝尔蒙特后，他向鲍西娅坦白了。鲍西娅看起来非常生气，发誓除非再见到那枚戒指，否则不会再理睬巴萨尼奥。但最后鲍西娅告诉巴萨尼奥，是自己假扮成律师，救了他朋友的命，并从他那里得到了戒指。于是，巴萨尼奥得到了原谅，他得知自己从匣子中抽到这么丰厚的奖赏，比以前更开心了。

第十二夜

伊利里亚公爵奥西诺深深地爱上了美丽的伯爵小姐奥丽维娅。然而，他所有的爱都是徒劳的，因为奥丽维娅不屑他的追求；奥丽维娅在哥哥死后，打发走了公爵派去的信使，要信使告诉主人，七年之内就算青天也不能窥见她的脸庞，她要像修女一样，戴着面纱行走；这一切做法都是为了把死去的哥哥的爱永远留在她悲伤的记忆中。

公爵渴望有一个他可以倾诉悲伤的对象，让他可以一遍又一遍地讲述他的爱情故事；碰巧就来了这样一个伙伴。大约就在这个时候，一艘船在伊利里亚海域失事了，在那些平安上岸的人中，有船长和一个名叫薇奥拉的美丽年轻的姑娘。但从海难中逃生并没有让她心存感激，因为她担心她的双胞胎哥哥西巴斯辛已经淹死了。对她来说，

TWELFTH·NIGHT.
OR
WHAT YOU WILL.

BURGESS

哥哥就像她胸膛里的心脏一样宝贵，他们是那么相像，要不是穿的衣服不同，别人很难把他们区分开。船长为了安慰她，告诉她说，他看到她哥哥把自己绑在"一根漂在海上的结实的桅杆上"，因此她哥哥有获救的希望。

薇奥拉打听她现在身处何处，她得知年轻的奥西诺公爵统治着这里，他的性格和他的名字一样高贵，于是她决定乔装成男子，去应聘做他的仆人。

她成功得到了这份工作，现在她每天都要听奥西诺讲爱情故事。起初，她非常同情奥西诺，但很快她的同情变成了爱情。最后，奥西诺想到，如果他派这个漂亮的小伙替他和奥丽维娅谈谈，他那毫无希望的求爱可能会有点进展。薇奥拉不情愿地去做这件事。她来到奥丽维娅家门口，她的管家马伏里奥，一个爱慕虚荣、爱管闲事、自爱过度的人，却不肯让她进去。

但是薇奥拉（现在叫西萨里奥）不接受自己被拒于门外，发誓一定要和伯爵小姐说上话。奥丽维娅听到有人违抗她的指令，很想看看这个勇敢的年轻人，她说："我们再听一听奥西诺的信使要说些什么。"

薇奥拉被带到她面前，她打发走仆人，耐心地听这位大胆的公爵信使责备她，结果她爱上了这个所谓的西萨里奥。西萨里奥走后，奥丽维娅想送给他一件礼物。于是，她叫来马伏里奥，命令他跟着那个小伙。

"他落下了这枚戒指，"说着，她从手指上取下戒指，"告诉他，我不要它。"

马伏里奥照她的吩咐去做了。当然，薇奥拉很清楚自己没有落下戒指，以女人敏锐的直觉，她知道奥丽维娅爱上了她。随后，她回到公爵身边，心里为她所爱的人、奥丽维娅，还有她自己难过。

她所能给予奥西诺的不过是无用的安慰，此时奥西诺正试图通过聆听甜美的音乐来减轻因爱情被轻视所受到的伤害，西萨里奥则站在他的身边。

"啊，"那天晚上，公爵对他的仆人说，"你也恋爱了。"

"略微有点。"薇奥拉回答。

"是个什么样子的女人？"他问道。

"容貌跟您差不多。"她回答。

"多大了？"他又问。

他得到了一个巧妙的回答："年纪跟您差不多，殿下。"

"太老了，天哪！"公爵叫道，"让这个女人嫁给一个比她年长的人吧。"

薇奥拉非常谦卑地回答："我觉得不错，殿下。"

不久，奥西诺再次恳求西萨里奥去探望奥丽维娅，代他表达爱意。但薇奥拉劝阻他说：

"如果有个女人像您爱奥丽维娅一样爱您呢？"

"啊！那是不可能的。"公爵说。

"但我很清楚，"薇奥拉继续说，"女人对男人会怀着什么样的爱情。我父亲有一个女儿，她爱上了一个男人，"她红着脸补充说，"正像如果我是一个女人，我也许会爱上殿下您的。"

"她的过去怎么样？"他问道。

"一片空白，殿下。"薇奥拉回答，"她从来不向人诉说她的爱情，而是让忧郁像藏在花蕾中的蛀虫一样，啃食她粉红的脸颊，她因相思而憔悴，坐在那里悲伤地微笑着。这难道不是爱吗？"

"可是你的妹妹没有殉情而死吧，我的孩子？"公爵问道。薇奥拉一直以这种机智的方法来表达自己对公爵的爱，她说：

"我父亲只有我这一个女儿，也只有我这一个儿子。殿下，我要不要去见这位小姐？"

"赶快去，"公爵说，立刻忘记了整个故事，"把这颗宝石给她。"

薇奥拉就这样去了。这一次，可怜的奥丽维娅无法掩饰她的爱，公开承认了，薇奥拉听了急忙离开她，说：

"我再也不代我的主人向您求爱了。"

但是在发誓的时候，薇奥拉并不知道她会对别人的痛苦心生温柔的怜悯。因此，当陷入爱情的奥丽维娅派出信使，祈求西萨里奥再来看望她时，西萨里奥便不忍心拒绝这个请求。

奥丽维娅对这名仆人的青睐引起了安德鲁·艾古契克爵士的嫉妒，安德鲁·艾古契克十分愚蠢，也曾遭到奥丽维娅的拒绝，当时他和奥丽维娅那位快乐的老叔叔托比爵士住在奥丽维娅家里。托比爵士非常喜欢搞恶作剧，他知道安德鲁爵士是个十足的懦夫，认为自己可以让安德鲁爵士和西萨里奥一决胜负。于是，他劝服安德鲁爵士向西萨里奥发出挑战，他还亲自把消息告诉西萨里奥。可怜的仆人非常惊恐，说：

"我还是回府吧，我不会跟人打架。"

"你不能回去，"托比爵士说，"除非你先和我打一架。"

托比看上去是一位非常凶狠的老先生，薇奥拉觉得最好还是等安德鲁爵士来。当安德鲁爵士终于出现时，薇奥拉吓得魂不守舍——因为担心真相败露，她只好颤抖地拔出了剑，安德鲁爵士也战战兢兢地跟着比画。幸好就在这个时候，一些警吏出现了，制止了他们打算进行的决斗。薇奥拉马上高兴地走开了，托比爵士在后面叫她：

"你是个懦夫！"

就在这些事情发生的时候，西巴斯辛已经脱离了所有的危险，安全抵达伊利里亚，他决定到公爵府去。在路上，就在薇奥拉匆忙离开的时候，他正经过奥丽维娅的家，他只见到了安德鲁爵士和托比爵士。安德鲁爵士误以为西巴斯辛是懦弱的西萨里奥，就鼓起勇气走到他跟前，给了他一拳，说："挨我一拳。"

"怎么，挨我这一拳，这一拳，这一拳！"西巴斯辛说，他狠狠地回敬了安德鲁爵士，打了他一拳又一拳，直到托比爵士来救他的朋友才停手。可是西巴斯辛挣脱了托比爵士的拉拽，拔剑想跟他们决斗，这时听到争吵声的奥丽维娅跑了过来，狠狠责备了托比爵士和他的朋友，并让他们离开。接着，她转向西巴斯辛，她误认为他是西萨里奥，请他一起到屋里去。

西巴斯辛被奥丽维娅的美貌和优雅所吸引，晕晕乎乎、满心欢喜，就欣然同意了。就在那天，在奥丽维娅发现他不是西萨里奥，也在西巴斯辛确定他不是在做梦之前，他们结婚了。

与此同时，奥西诺听说西萨里奥与奥丽维娅谈得不好，决定带着西萨里奥亲自拜访奥丽维娅。奥丽维娅在家门口遇到了他们，她以为那是她丈夫，就责怪西萨里奥离她而去，并对公爵说，公爵的追求让她厌恶。

"仍旧那么残忍吗？"奥西诺说。

"仍旧那么坚定。"她回答。

奥西诺从愤怒变得残酷，他发誓，为了报复奥丽维娅，他要杀了西萨里奥，他知道奥丽维娅爱西萨里奥。"来吧，孩子。"他对仆人说。

薇奥拉跟着他走了，说："我，为了让您内心安宁，宁愿死上一千次。"

奥丽维娅非常害怕，她大声喊道："西萨里奥，我的丈夫，别走！"

"她的丈夫？"公爵生气地问道。

"不，殿下，我不是。"薇奥拉说。

"请神父来。"奥丽维娅叫道。

为西巴斯辛和奥丽维娅主婚的神父进来了，他称西萨里奥就是新郎。

"啊，你这个骗子！"公爵叫道，"别了，你带她走吧，去你我以后再也不会相遇的地方。"

就在这时，安德鲁爵士头破血流地走过来，他抱怨西萨里奥打破了他的头，也打伤了托比爵士。

"我从来没有伤害过你，"薇奥拉非常坚定地说，"你拔剑向我，但我跑开了，没有伤害你。"

尽管她一直在抗议，却没有人相信她；这时，西巴斯辛进来了，所有人都震惊了。

"对不起，夫人，"他对妻子说，"我伤害了你的亲戚。对不起，亲爱的，即便我们不久之前才对彼此立下盟誓。"

"一样的面孔，一样的声音，一样的习惯，却是两个人！"公爵叫道，他先看看薇奥拉，又看看西巴斯辛。

"一个苹果切成两半，"一个认识西巴斯辛的人说，

"也不会比这两个人更为相像了。哪个是西巴斯辛呢？"

"我从来没有兄弟，"西巴斯辛说，"我只有一个妹妹，她已经被汹涌的巨浪吞噬了。如果你是个女人，"他对薇奥拉说，"我就会让眼泪落在你的脸颊上，并且说：'欢迎你，淹死了的薇奥拉！'"

薇奥拉很高兴看到她亲爱的哥哥还活着，承认自己确实是他的妹妹薇奥拉。她这样说的时候，奥西诺感到了一种类似于爱情的怜悯。

"小伙子，"他说，"你对我说过一千次，你爱上了一个和我很像的女子。"

"我发誓那些话都是真的。"薇奥拉回答。

"把手给我，"奥西诺高兴地叫道，"你将成为我的妻子。"

于是，温柔的薇奥拉快乐起来，奥丽维娅发现西巴斯辛是个专一的情人，一个好丈夫，而她是个真诚而有爱心的妻子。

皆大欢喜

从前有个邪恶的公爵叫弗莱德里克，他夺走了本应属于他哥哥的领土，并把他哥哥流放了。他的哥哥进入亚登森林，在那里过着无畏的林中人的生活，就像昔日罗宾汉在快活的英格兰的舍伍德森林里一样。

被放逐公爵的女儿罗瑟琳和弗莱德里克的女儿西莉娅住在一起，她们比大多数姐妹更要好。有一天，宫廷里办了一场摔跤比赛，罗瑟琳和西莉娅去看比赛。查尔斯是著名的摔跤手，曾有很多人在比赛中死在他手下。要和他搏斗的青年奥兰多，看起来那么单薄年轻。罗瑟琳和西莉娅认为他肯定会跟其他人一样丢掉性命。于是她们劝奥兰多不要尝试如此危险的比赛；结果适得其反，这让奥兰多更希望在这场比赛中表现出色，从而赢得可爱小姐们的

AS YOU LIKE IT

赞美。

奥兰多和罗瑟琳的父亲一样，被自己的哥哥剥夺了继承权，他为哥哥的不仁感到非常难过，直到见到罗瑟琳之前，他都不关心自己的生死。但现在看到美丽的罗瑟琳，他有了力量和勇气，所以表现得很出色，最后他把查尔斯重重地摔倒在地。弗莱德里克公爵十分赞赏他的勇气，问他叫什么名字。

"我叫奥兰多，我是罗兰·德·鲍埃爵士的小儿子。"年轻人说。

罗兰·德·鲍埃爵士在世的时候和被放逐的公爵是好友。弗莱德里克听到奥兰多是谁的儿子后，很是遗憾，就不愿意再结识他了。罗瑟琳听说这位英俊年轻的陌生人是她父亲老友的儿子，却很高兴。她们要离开的时候，她不止一次转过身来，对这位勇敢的年轻人说几句亲切的话。

"先生，"她说着，从脖子上取下一条项链递给他，"为了我，请戴上它吧。"

罗瑟琳和西莉娅单独在一起时，开始谈论那名英俊的摔跤手，罗瑟琳承认自己对他一见钟情。

"得啦，得啦，"西莉娅说，"跟你的爱情较劲吧。"

"噢，"罗瑟琳回答说，"它比我力气大。你看，公爵来了。"

"他的眼睛里充满了怒气。"西莉娅说。

"你必须马上离开宫廷。"他对罗瑟琳说。

"为什么？"她问道。

"别问为什么，"公爵回答说，"你被放逐了。十天之内，要是在离我们宫廷二十英里之内的地方发现你，你就得死。"

于是，罗瑟琳出发去亚登森林寻找她的父亲，那位被放逐的公爵。西莉娅太爱她了，不让她一个人去。这是一段相当危险的旅程，罗瑟琳个子高些，就乔装成年轻的男子，她的堂妹打扮成乡下姑娘。罗瑟琳说她叫盖米亚德，西莉娅说她叫爱怜娜。她们终于抵达亚登森林时，已经非常疲惫了。她们坐在草地上，一名农夫从那里经过，盖米亚德问农夫能不能给她们弄点吃的。农夫照做了，并告诉她们一个牧羊人正在出售羊群和屋子。她们买下羊群和屋子，在森林里当起牧羊人。

与此同时，奥列佛试图夺去他弟弟奥兰多的性命，奥兰多因此也走进森林，他在那里遇到了长公爵，受到亲切的接待，便住下来。现在，奥兰多心里只想着罗瑟琳，他在森林里游逛，在树上刻下她的名字，又写下一首首情诗，挂在灌木上。罗瑟琳和西莉娅看到了它们。有一天，奥兰多遇见了她俩，但罗瑟琳穿着男装，他没认出来，不过他很喜欢这个漂亮的牧羊青年，因为他觉得牧羊青年长得很像罗瑟琳。

"有一个愚蠢的爱恋者，"罗瑟琳说，"常在这树林里出没，把十四行诗挂在树上。如果我能找到他，我会很快治好他的蠢病。"

奥兰多承认他就是那个愚蠢的爱恋者，罗瑟琳说："如果你每天都来见我，我就假装是罗瑟琳。我会扮成她，像大多数女人一样，时而任性时而乖巧，直到你为爱她这一愚蠢行为感到羞耻为止。"

就这样，奥兰多每天都去她的住处，把他想对罗瑟琳说的所有动听的话都说给她听，并以此为乐。罗瑟琳亲耳听到了奥兰多所有的情话，心里暗暗高兴。就这样，他们愉快地度过了很多天。

一天早晨，奥兰多正要去见盖米亚德时，看见一个人躺在地上睡着了，旁边卧着一只母狮，在等睡着的人醒来：因为人们说，狮子不会捕食任何死去或睡着之物。奥兰多端详这个人，发现正是他邪恶的哥哥奥列佛，那曾试图要他命的人。他和母狮搏斗，杀死了母狮，救了奥列佛一命。

奥兰多与母狮搏斗时，奥列佛醒来看到了他的弟弟。他对弟弟不好，弟弟却冒着生命危险从野兽爪下救下他。这使他为自己的恶行后悔，他请求奥兰多原谅他，从此以后，他们成了亲密的兄弟。母狮伤了奥兰多的胳膊，奥兰多不能继续去见牧羊人了，于是他让哥哥去请盖米亚德过来。

奥列佛把整个故事告诉了盖米亚德和爱怜娜，爱怜娜被他那种男子汉气概的坦白方式迷住了，立刻爱上了他。但盖米亚德听说奥兰多身处危险时，晕倒了；苏醒过来后，她诚恳地说："我理应是个女人。"

奥列佛回到弟弟身边，把这一切都告诉了他，又说："我太爱爱怜娜了，我愿意把我的财产给你，然后娶她为妻，在这里当个牧羊人。"

"你们就在明天举行婚礼吧，"奥兰多说，"我会邀请公爵和他的朋友们过来的。"

奥兰多告诉盖米亚德，他的哥哥第二天将结婚，他补充道："哦，从别人的眼中看到幸福是多么令人苦闷。"

罗瑟琳仍然穿着盖米亚德的衣服，她用盖米亚德的声音说："如果你真的如此深爱罗瑟琳，那么当你哥哥和爱怜娜结婚时，你会娶罗瑟琳吧。"

第二天，长公爵和他的随从们，还有奥兰多、奥列佛和爱怜娜，都来相聚参加婚礼。

随后，盖米亚德进来对长公爵说："如果我把您的女儿罗瑟琳带来，您愿意把她交给奥兰多吗？"长公爵说："即使我有万国作为她的陪嫁，我也愿意。"

"你说过，我带她来，你就会娶她？"她又对奥兰多说。奥兰多回答："即使我是万国的君王，我也愿意。"

然后，罗瑟琳和西莉娅出去了，过了一会儿回来时，罗瑟琳换上了漂亮的女装。

她转向父亲，说："我把自己交给您，因为我是您的。"长公爵说："如果眼见为实，那么你就是我的女儿。"

接着，她对奥兰多说："我把自己交给你，因为我是你的。"奥兰多说："如果眼见为实，那么你就是我的罗瑟琳。"

"如果您不是我父亲，那么我就没有父亲。"她对长公爵说，然后又对奥兰多说，"如果你不是我丈夫，我就没有丈夫。"

就这样，奥兰多和罗瑟琳结婚了，奥列佛也和西莉娅结婚了，他们从此生活幸福，并和长公爵一起回到了公国。一位隐士将弗莱德里克的恶行指明给他，所以他把公国还给了哥哥，自己到修道院去祈求宽恕了。

婚礼在长满青苔的林间空地举行，气氛十分欢乐。一对牧羊人和牧羊女跟他们在同一天举行了婚礼，他们是罗瑟琳扮成牧羊人时认识的朋友。宴会和狂欢这一切只能在美丽的绿树林里享受到，任何室内场所都无法提供这样的欢娱。

无事生非

西西里岛上有一座叫墨西拿的小镇，几百年前，这里发生了一件小题大做的稀奇事。

开始是非常愉快的。西班牙的阿拉贡亲王唐·彼德罗打败了敌人，取得了彻底的胜利，以至于人们忘记了他们来自什么地方。在经历了令人疲惫的战争之后，唐·彼德罗心情愉快，来到墨西拿度假。随行人员中有他同父异母的弟弟唐·约翰与两名年轻的意大利贵族，培尼狄克和克劳狄奥。

培尼狄克是个快活的话匣子，他决心当个单身汉。与他截然不同的是，克劳狄奥一到奥墨西拿，就爱上了墨西拿总督里奥那托的女儿希罗。

七月的一天，一名叫波拉契奥的香料师正在里奥那托

MUCH ADO About NOTHING.

家里一间发霉的房间里烧干的薰衣草，这时从敞开的窗户飘来了谈话的声音。

"跟我说说你对希罗的明智看法。"克劳狄奥问道。为了听得更清楚，波拉契奥停下手里的工作。

"太矮了，肤色太深了，不能让人赞扬她，"培尼狄克回答说，"可是如果改变她的肤色或身高，那还不如现在漂亮。"

"在我看来，她是最可爱的女人。"克劳狄奥说。

培尼狄克反驳道："我不需要戴眼镜，可是我也瞧不出来她有什么可爱。如果你把她放在她堂姐旁边，那堂姐就像五月初始，而她就像十二月的岁暮。可惜的是，贝特丽丝小姐是个暴脾气。"

贝特丽丝是里奥那托的侄女。培尼狄克管她叫"尖嘴小姐"，而她以既诙谐又严厉地说培尼狄克的坏话为乐。她常说她出生在一颗跳舞的星星下，因此不会迟钝无趣。

克劳狄奥和培尼狄克还在说话，这时唐·彼德罗走过来，打趣道："喂，先生们，在讲什么秘密？"

培尼狄克回答："我很希望殿下命令我说出来。"

"那么，我命令你忠实地告诉我。"唐·彼德罗幽默地说。

"我可以像哑巴一样不说话，"培尼狄克向克劳狄奥道歉，"但殿下命令我说话。"他对唐·彼德罗说："克劳狄奥爱上了希罗，里奥那托的矮女儿。"

唐·彼德罗很高兴，因为他欣赏希罗，也很喜欢克劳狄奥。培尼狄克走后，他对克劳狄奥说："你要坚定地爱希罗，我会帮你赢得她的。今晚她的父亲要举办一场化装舞会，我就化装冒充你，告诉她克劳狄奥多爱她。如果她心生喜悦，我就去找她父亲，请求他同意你们的婚事。"

大多数男人都喜欢自己求婚，但如果你爱上了总督的独生女，那么有能信任的亲王为你求情，你就太幸运了。

克劳狄奥是幸运的，但也是不幸的，因为他有一个敌人，但表面上是他的朋友。这人就是唐·彼德罗同父异母的弟弟唐·约翰，他嫉妒克劳狄奥，因为唐·彼德罗更喜欢克劳狄奥而不是他。

波拉契奥把他听到的有趣谈话告诉了唐·约翰。

"我也去那场化装舞会找找乐子。"波拉契奥讲完后，唐·约翰说。

化装舞会当晚，唐·彼德罗戴着面具，假装自己是克劳狄奥，问希罗自己是否可以和她一起散步。

他们一起走了，唐·约翰走到克劳狄奥面前说："我想您是培尼狄克先生吧？""正是。"克劳狄奥撒谎说。

唐·约翰说："如果您能利用您对我哥哥的影响来消除他对希罗的爱，我将非常感激。希罗的地位配不上他。"

"您怎么知道他爱希罗呢？"克劳狄奥问道。

"我听见他发誓说很爱她。"唐·约翰回答。波拉契奥附和道："我也听到了。"

克劳狄奥独自一人离开了，他觉得亲王背叛了他。"再见了，希罗，"他喃喃地说，"我真是个傻瓜，竟然相信可以请人代劳。"

与此同时，贝特丽丝和培尼狄克（他戴着面具）正在热烈地交换意见。

"培尼狄克曾经让您笑过吗？"她问道。

"培尼狄克是谁？"他问道。

"亲王的弄臣。"贝特丽丝回答。她说话如此尖刻，以至于后来培尼狄克说："即使她的嫁妆是伊甸园，我也不会娶她。"

但化装舞会上说话最多的既不是贝特丽丝，也不是培尼狄克，而是唐·彼德罗。他严格执行了他的计划，之后和里奥那托及希罗一起出现在克劳狄奥面前，他说："克劳狄奥，你预备什么时候去教堂？"刹那间，克劳狄奥的脸上重现了光彩。

"明天，"克劳狄奥迅速回答，"在我迎娶希罗之前，时间走得像一个拄拐杖的跛子一样慢。"

"给她一周吧，我亲爱的贤婿。"里奥那托说，克劳狄奥的心因为喜悦而怦怦直跳。

"现在，"和蔼的唐·彼德罗说，"我们必须为培尼狄克先生寻个妻子。这可是大力神赫拉克勒斯的任务。"

"即使要我十个晚上不睡觉，"里奥那托说，"我也愿意相助。"

随后，希罗说："殿下，我也愿意尽微薄之力为贝特丽丝找个好丈夫。"

就这样，化装舞会在愉快的笑声中结束了，克劳狄奥并没有得到教训。

波拉契奥向唐·约翰提出了一个计划，他相信这个计划可以让克劳狄奥和唐·彼德罗相信希罗是个脚踏两条船的不贞女子。唐·约翰很高兴，同意了这个充满仇恨的计划。

与此同时，唐·彼德罗设计了一个巧妙的爱情计划。"如果，"他对里奥那托说，"贝特丽丝在附近无意中听到我们说话时，我们假装在谈论培尼狄克渴望她的爱，她就会同情培尼狄克，看到他的优点，从而爱上他。如果培尼狄克认为我们不知道他在听，而我们故意说，美丽的贝特丽丝竟会爱上像培尼狄克这样无情的讥笑者，这是多么可悲，那么培尼狄克肯定会在一周或更短的时间内跪在她面前。"

所以有一天，培尼狄克在凉亭读书时，克劳狄奥和里奥那托坐在外面说："你女儿告诉我，她写了一封信。"

"信！"里奥那托大声叫道，"她夜里会起来二十次，天知道在写些什么。希罗瞥了一眼，看到纸上写着'培尼狄克和贝特丽丝'，然后贝特丽丝就把纸撕了。"

"希罗告诉我，"克劳狄奥说，"她喊道，'哦，可爱的培尼狄克！'"

培尼狄克被这个不可思议的故事深深打动了，他自负地信以为真。"她漂亮又善良，"他心里说，"我可不能显得傲慢。我觉得我爱她。人们一定会讥笑我，但他们的纸子弹伤害不了我。"

这时，贝特丽丝来到凉亭，说："我违背自己的意愿来告诉你，晚饭已经准备好了。"

"美丽的贝特丽丝，谢谢你。"培尼狄克说。

"我不费什么力气就来了，就像你不费什么力气谢我一样。"对方回答，想让他难堪。

但这并没有让他难堪，反而让他觉得暖心。他从贝特丽丝那粗鲁的话语中体会出来的意思是，贝特丽丝很高兴来叫他。

希罗负责融化贝特丽丝的心，她不费力就找到了机会。有一天，她只是对女仆玛格莱特说："你快跑到客厅去，悄悄告诉贝特丽丝，我和欧苏拉正在果园里谈论她。"

说了这番话，她觉得贝特丽丝一定会偷听她的谈话，就像她和她的堂姐约好了一样。

果园里有一座凉亭，隐在忍冬的阴凉里，玛格莱特办完差事几分钟后，贝特丽丝就走进了凉亭。

"可是您能肯定，"希罗的侍女欧苏拉问，"培尼狄克一心一意地爱着贝特丽丝吗？"

"亲王和克劳狄奥也这么说，"希罗回答，"他们希望我告诉她，但我说，'不！让培尼狄克努力斩断情丝吧。'"

"您为什么要这么说呢？"

"因为贝特丽丝无比骄傲。她的眼睛里闪烁着鄙视和轻蔑的光。她太骄傲了，根本不屑去恋爱。我不希望看到她玩弄可怜的培尼狄克的爱。我宁愿看到培尼狄克的爱像被压住的火一样，慢慢熄灭。"

"我不同意您的观点，"欧苏拉说，"我认为您的堂姐头脑很清楚，不会看不出培尼狄克的优点。"

"在意大利，除了克劳狄奥，就数他了。"希罗说。

谈话者离开了果园，贝特丽丝激动而温柔地走出凉亭，自言自语道："可怜的、亲爱的培尼狄克，一直忠于我吧，你的爱会驯服我这颗狂野的心。"

我们再说说那份仇恨的计划。

克劳狄奥婚礼的前一天晚上，唐·约翰走进房间，唐·彼德罗和克劳狄奥正在谈话，他问克劳狄奥是否打算明天结婚。

"你知道他打算啊！"唐·彼德罗说。

唐·约翰说："如果他跟着我，看到我想给他看的，他可能就会有不同的看法。"

他们跟着唐·约翰走进花园，看见一个女子从希罗的窗户探出身来，和波拉契奥谈情说爱。

克劳狄奥认为那个女子是希罗，说："我明天会让她为此羞愧！"唐·彼德罗也认为她是希罗。但那不是希罗，而是玛格莱特。

克劳狄奥和唐·彼德罗离开花园时，唐·约翰轻声笑起来。他给了波拉契奥一只装着一千金币的钱袋。

这笔钱让波拉契奥很得意，和朋友康拉德走在街上时，他便夸耀自己的财富和财富的赠予者，并说出了自己的所作所为。

一个巡夜人听到了他们的谈话，觉得他应该收押一个因为做坏事而得到一千金币报酬的人。因此，他逮捕了波拉契奥和康拉德，他们在监狱里度过了那晚。

第二天中午之前，墨西拿一半的贵族来到教堂。希罗想这是她的婚礼，所以穿着婚纱出现，她美丽的脸庞上、坦率闪亮的眼睛里都没有一丝阴霾。

主持婚礼的是法兰西斯神父。

他转向克劳狄奥说："爵爷，您是来这里结婚这位小姐吗？""不！"克劳狄奥反对道。

里奥那托以为他是在语法问题上吹毛求疵。"您应该说，神父，"他说，"您是来娶她的。"

法兰西斯神父转向了希罗。"小姐，"他说，"您是来这里嫁给这位伯爵吗？""是的。"希罗回答。

"要是你俩有谁知道这桩婚姻有什么障碍，我命令你们说出来。"神父说。

"你知道有吗，希罗？"克劳狄奥问道。"没有。"希罗说。

"您知道有吗，伯爵？"神父问道。"我敢替他回答'没有'。"里奥那托说。

克劳狄奥痛苦地叫道："哦！有什么是人们不敢说的呢！神父。"他继续说："您愿意把女儿给我吗？"里奥那托回答："就像上帝把她给我一样愿意。"

"我能给您什么，"克劳狄奥问，"它的价值能抵得过这份礼物？""什么都不行，"唐·彼德罗说，"除非您把这份礼物仍旧还给赠予人。"

"尊敬的殿下，您教会我了，"克劳狄奥说，"好了，里奥那托，把她领回去吧。"

紧接着，克劳狄奥、唐·彼德罗和唐·约翰又说了一些粗野的话。

教堂似乎不再神圣了。希罗尽她所能地为自己辩护，后来她晕倒了。迫害她的人都离开了教堂，她的父亲留下了。他被希罗受到的那些指控蒙蔽了，大声喊道："让她去死！"

但是法兰西斯神父用他那双洞察灵魂的敏锐眼睛看出了希罗是清白的，他说："有一千种迹象告诉我她是清白的。"

希罗在他亲切的目光下醒过来。她的父亲又急又气，不知如何是好。神父说："他们离开的时候，以为她已经蒙羞而死了。那就让我们假装她已经死了，直等到真相大白，中伤变成悔恨。"

"神父的建议很好。"培尼狄克说。希罗被带到一个僻静的地方，贝特丽丝和培尼狄克独自留在教堂里。

培尼狄克知道贝特丽丝痛哭了很久很久。"我相信你那善良的堂妹一定是被冤枉的。"他说。可她仍然在哭泣。

"这不是很奇怪吗？"培尼狄克温和地问道，"你是我在这世上最爱的人。"

"我也可以说，你是我在这世上最爱的人，"贝特丽丝说，"但我不说出来。我为堂妹感到难过。"

"告诉我，我能为她做点什么。"培尼狄克说。"杀了克劳狄奥。"贝特丽丝说。

"哈！那可办不到。"培尼狄克说。"您拒绝我，就是杀了我，"贝特丽丝说，"再见了。"

"够了！我要去向他提出挑战。"培尼狄克叫道。

这一幕中，波拉契奥和康拉德身在狱中，一个叫道格培里的警吏在审讯他们。

巡夜人作证说，波拉契奥曾说他因为密谋陷害希罗而得到了一千金币。

里奥那托没有出席这次审讯，但现在他完全相信希罗是无辜的。他很好地扮演了痛失爱女的父亲的角色，当唐·彼德罗和克劳狄奥友好地来拜访他时，他对这个意大利人说："你中伤我的孩子，使她蒙羞而死，我要跟你决斗。"

"我不能和一位老人打架。"克劳狄奥说。

"你却可以杀死一个女孩。"里奥那托冷笑道。克劳狄奥的脸红了。

他们越说言辞越激烈。里奥那托离开房间，培尼狄克进来了，唐·彼德罗和克劳狄奥都感到自己如同被放在火上炙烤。

"那老头，"克劳狄奥说，"想把我的鼻子咬掉。"

"你是个混蛋！"培尼狄克简短地说，"你喜欢什么时候，用什么武器跟我决斗都可以，你要是不应战，我就叫你懦夫。"

克劳狄奥很震惊，说："我一定奉陪。谁也不能说我没办法把小牛的头砍掉。"

培尼狄克笑了，现在是唐·彼德罗接见警吏的时候了。亲王坐在王座上，准备主持公正。

门很快开了，道格培里和他看押的囚犯们走进来。

唐·彼德罗问："这些人犯了什么罪？"

波拉契奥把全部责任都推给逃走了的唐·约翰。"希罗小姐已经死了，"他说，"我只求一死，这是一个凶手应得的。"

克劳狄奥听完后，感到痛苦，深深懊悔。

里奥那托回来时，克劳狄奥就对他说："这个奴隶证明您女儿是清白的。您选择报复的方式吧。"

"里奥那托，"唐·彼德罗谦恭地说，"我已经准备好接受您的任何惩罚了。"

"那么，我请你们俩，"里奥那托说，"宣告我女儿是清白的，并在她的墓前唱赞美她的诗歌以纪念她。至于你，克劳狄奥，我想说的是：我弟弟有一个女儿和希罗简直一模一样。你要是和她结婚，我的仇恨就平息了。"

"尊敬的老人家，"克劳狄奥说，"我愿意听从您的驱使。"之后，克劳狄奥走进房间，写了一首肃穆的诗歌。克劳狄奥跟着唐·彼德罗和他的随从们一起去了教堂，在里奥那托家族的墓碑前唱了这首诗歌。唱完，他说："再见，希罗。我每年都会这样做的。"

于是，他心情沉重地准备娶一个他不爱的姑娘，他的心已经给了希罗。他获知要到里奥那托家去见她后，如约而至。

他被带进了一个房间，安东尼奥（里奥那托的弟弟）走进房间，后面跟着几位戴面具的小姐。法兰西斯神父、里奥那托和培尼狄克都在场。

安东尼奥领着其中一位小姐走向克劳狄奥。

"亲爱的，"年轻人说，"让我看看你的芳容吧。"

"你先发誓娶她。"里奥那托说。

"给我你的手，"克劳狄奥对那位小姐说，"在这位神圣的神父面前，我发誓，如果你愿意做我的妻子，我就娶你。"

"我活着就是你的妻子。"女子说着摘下了面具。

"另一个希罗！"克劳狄奥叫道。

里奥那托解释说："只有在谣言流传的时候，希罗才是死的。"

神父打算为这对重归于好的情侣主持婚礼，但培尼狄克打断了他的话："且慢，神父，这些小姐中哪一位是贝特丽丝？"

现在，贝特丽丝取下面具。培尼狄克说："你爱我，是不是？"

"一般。"对方回答，"你爱我吗？"

"一般。"培尼狄克回答。

"我听说你对我很专一。"贝特丽丝说。

“我也得到了同样的消息。”培尼狄克说。

“这是你自己的笔迹，证明了你的爱。”克劳狄奥说着，拿出了一首蹩脚的十四行诗，那是培尼狄克写给他的心上人的。“这，”希罗说，“是献给培尼狄克的诗，是我从贝特丽丝的口袋里拿出来的。”

“真是个奇迹！”培尼狄克叫道，“我们的手违背了我们的心！好吧，我愿意娶你，贝特丽丝。”

“我嫁给你，也只是为了救你一命。”对方回答说。

培尼狄克吻住了贝特丽丝的嘴。在为克劳狄奥和希罗主持婚礼后，神父也给他们主持了婚礼。

“结婚后的培尼狄克怎么样了？”唐·彼德罗问道。

“高兴到不会感到难过，”培尼狄克回答，“我才不理会那些冷嘲热讽的话。至于你，克劳狄奥，我本来打算和你打一架的，但你现在是我的亲戚了，你就安然生活，好好地爱我的小姨子吧。”

“直到今天，我的棍棒可一直想打你一顿呢，培尼狄克。”克劳狄奥说。“来吧，来吧，我们跳舞。”培尼狄克却说。

他们跳起舞来。即使是唐·约翰被抓获的消息也不能使幸福的恋人们停下飞扬的舞步，因为对一个没有造成伤害的坏人复仇是没有意义的。

暴风雨

米兰公爵普洛斯帕罗是一个博学勤奋的人，他整天埋头读书，把公国的事务交给他的弟弟安东尼奥管理，他完全信任安东尼奥。但这种信任没有得到应有的回报，安东尼奥想亲自戴上公爵的冠冕。为了达到目的，要不是顾忌人们对他的爱戴，他甚至要杀了他的哥哥。然而，在普洛斯帕罗的敌人，那不勒斯国王阿朗索的帮助下，他设法把公国及其所有的荣誉、权力和财富掌握在了自己手中。他们把普洛斯帕罗带到海上，在远离陆地的时候，强迫他坐上一条没有渔具、桅杆和帆的小船。出于残忍和仇恨，他们把普洛斯帕罗的小女儿米兰达（还不到三岁）和他一起带到小船上，然后他们扬帆离去，让父女俩听天由命。

但安东尼奥的一名侍臣对他的故主普洛斯帕罗很忠

CASSELL'S ILLUSTRATED SHAKESPEARE

THE TEMPEST.

诚。要把公爵从敌人手中救出来是不可能的，但他做了很多事情来表达他身为臣子的爱。这位名叫贡札罗的可敬的勋爵，偷偷在船上放了一些淡水、食物和衣服，以及普洛斯帕罗最珍视的东西，他的一些珍贵的书。

小船漂到了一个小岛，普洛斯帕罗和他的孩子安全登陆。这个岛被施了魔法，多年来一直处于恶女巫西考拉克斯咒语的控制下，她把在那里发现的所有善良的精灵都囚禁在树干里。在普洛斯帕罗被抛弃在这片海岸之上前不久，她死去了，但精灵的首领爱丽儿仍然被囚禁着。

普洛斯帕罗是一位了不起的魔法师，因为他在让弟弟管理米兰的事务的那些年里，一直潜心研究魔法。他用魔法释放了被囚禁的精灵们，又使他们服从他的意旨，他们比米兰的子民更像他真正的臣民。只要他们遵从他的命令，他就善待他们，并且他对他们行使权力既明智又妥善。只有一个人，他觉得必须严厉对待，那就是老巫婆的儿子卡列班，一个丑陋、畸形的怪物，长得很可怕，而且他的所有习性都恶毒而残忍。

米兰达长成一个美丽可爱的少女时，碰巧安东尼奥和阿朗索、他的弟弟塞巴斯蒂安、他的儿子费迪南德，还有老贡札罗一起在海上航行，他们的船驶近了普洛斯帕罗所在的岛。普洛斯帕罗知道他们来了，就用魔法掀起了一场大风暴，甚至船上的水手也以为自己要完蛋了。费迪南德王子率先跳进大海，他父亲认为他淹死了，悲痛万分。但其实爱丽儿把他安全地带上了岸；其余的船员虽然被冲到海里，但也都安然无恙地在小岛的不同地方登陆，他们都以为船已经损毁了，但那艘船也完好无损，爱丽儿把船带到港口，停泊在那里。普洛斯帕罗和他的精灵们创造了这样的奇迹。

暴风雨还在肆虐的时候，普洛斯帕罗让女儿看那艘在海浪里挣扎的勇敢的船，并告诉她船上载满了像他们一样的活人。她可怜那些生命，祈求掀起这场风暴的人让它平息下来。父亲叫她不要害怕，因为他打算拯救他们每一个人。

他第一次把他们的经历告诉女儿，说他掀起这场风暴，是为了捕获他的敌人安东尼奥和阿朗索。

他讲完故事后，用魔法使女儿睡着了，因为爱丽儿在他身边，他有工作要给爱丽儿做。爱丽儿渴望获得完全的自由，抱怨他的差事很苦，但一想到他在西考拉克斯统治这片土地时遭受的种种苦难，以及他对结束那些苦难的主人的感激之情，他就不再抱怨，而是忠实地执行普洛斯帕罗的任何命令。

"照做吧，"普洛斯帕罗说，"两天后我就给你自由。"

然后，他吩咐爱丽儿扮作水中仙子，去寻找年轻的王子。爱丽儿在费迪南德身边盘旋、歌唱，费迪南德却看不见他。

费迪南德跟着神奇的歌声游，歌声变得庄严肃穆，他心中充满了悲伤，眼里噙满了泪水。

爱丽儿就这样唱着，引领被迷住的王子来到普洛斯帕罗和米兰达面前。看！一切都如普洛斯帕罗所愿。自从米兰达记事以来，除了父亲以外，从来没有见过任何人，她用崇敬的眼神看着这位年轻的王子，内心暗暗充满爱意。

"我简直要说，"她说，"他是位神，因为我从没见过自然之中有这么高贵的人！"

费迪南德看到她的美貌，又惊又喜，感叹道：

"我敢肯定，这一定是这些曲子所歌唱的那位女神了！"

他并不试图掩饰米兰达在他心中引燃的热情，没说几句话，他就发誓，如果米兰达愿意，他就迎娶米兰达为王后。普洛斯帕罗虽然暗自高兴，却装出愤怒的样子。

"你是来打探消息的。"他对费迪南德说，"我要把你的头和脚锁在一起。你只能吃河蚌、干枯的树根和种子的皮壳，只能喝海水。跟我来。"

"不。"费迪南德说着拔出了剑。但普洛斯帕罗立刻施法迷住他，使他像雕像一样站在那里，像石头一样一动不动。米兰达害怕了，祈祷父亲宽恕她的情人。但父亲严厉地拒绝了米兰达，让费迪南德跟着他来到牢房。在那里，他让王子干活，让王子把数千根沉重的木头堆起来；费迪南德耐心地服从了，他认为他虽辛劳，但得到亲爱的米兰达的同情，就是很好的补偿了。

米兰达非常同情他，本想帮他干点苦活，可是他不让米兰达这样做，不过他不能对米兰达隐瞒爱意，米兰达听了很高兴，答应做他的妻子。

普洛斯帕罗打心底高兴，解除了他的劳役，同意他们结婚。

"带她走吧，"他说，"她是你的了。"

与此同时，安东尼奥和塞巴斯蒂安在岛上的另一个地方密谋杀死那不勒斯国王阿朗索，因为他们认为费迪南德死了，如果阿朗索也死了，塞巴斯蒂安就能继承王位。他们本想趁受害者睡着的时候实现邪恶的目的，但爱丽儿及时把阿朗索叫醒了。

爱丽儿耍了很多把戏。他在他们面前摆了一桌宴席，正当他们准备享用时，突然电闪雷鸣，他以女妖的形象出现，宴席立刻消失了。爱丽儿指责他们犯了罪，随后也消失了。

普洛斯帕罗用魔法把他们引到小树林里，他们在那里等待时害怕得浑身颤抖，终于痛苦地悔罪了。

普洛斯帕罗决定最后一次使用魔法。"之后，"他说，"我要折断魔杖，把书投进水里。"

说完，他施法让空中响起仙乐，他以米兰公爵的样子出现在大家面前。既然他们忏悔了，他便原谅了他们，并讲述了自从他们残忍地把他和小女儿交给风浪摆布以后他的生活经历。阿朗索似乎对自己过去的罪行最为悔恨，同时他痛惜失去了继承人。普洛斯帕罗拉开帘子，让他们看到费迪南德和米兰达正在下棋。阿朗索很高兴再次见到心爱的儿子，当听说和费迪南德一起下棋的漂亮姑娘是普洛斯帕罗的女儿，而且这对年轻人已经订婚了，他说：

　　"让我握住你们的手，谁不希望你们快乐，就让悲伤和懊悔永远攫住他的心。"

　　就这样，一切都圆满结束了。船安然无恙地停泊在港口，第二天他们就出发去那不勒斯，费迪南德和米兰达将在那里举行婚礼。爱丽儿以平静的大海和有利的大风助他们远行。

　　普洛斯帕罗在离开多年后，回到了自己的公国，在那里他受到了忠实臣民的热烈欢迎。他不再使用魔法，但他的生活很幸福，因为他恢复了往日的生活，更因为当曾经对他造成致命伤害的最恶毒的敌人落入他手中时，他没有报复他们，而是高尚地原谅了他们。

　　至于爱丽儿，普洛斯帕罗让他像空气一样自由，他可以去他想去的任何地方，怀着轻松的心情唱出甜美的歌。

冬天的故事

列昂特斯是西西里的国王，他最亲密的朋友波力克希尼斯是波希米亚的国王。他们一起长大，直到各自去统治自己的王国时才分开。多年以后，当两人都结婚并有了一个儿子时，波力克希尼斯来到西西里和列昂特斯住在一起。

列昂特斯是个脾气暴躁又愚笨的人，他愚蠢地认为妻子赫美温妮喜欢波力克希尼斯，而不是自己的丈夫。一旦他有了这种想法，就没有什么能把它消除了。他命令大臣卡密罗在波力克希尼斯的酒里下毒。卡密罗试图劝阻他这么做，但发现他不为所动，就假装同意了。然后，卡密罗告诉波力克希尼斯列昂特斯要对付他，于是他们那天晚上逃离西西里宫廷，回到了波希米亚。在那里，卡密罗作为

THE WINTER'S TALE

波力克希尼斯的朋友和公使继续生活。

列昂特斯把王后投进监狱。她的儿子，王位继承人，看到母亲受到如此不公正和残忍的对待，悲伤而死。

王后在监狱中生下了一个孩子，她的朋友宝琳娜给婴儿穿上最漂亮的衣服，带去给国王看，期望国王看到无助的小女儿之后会对亲爱的王后心软。王后从来没有辜负过国王，她对国王的爱远远超过了国王应得的。但国王不愿看孩子一眼，命令宝琳娜的丈夫把孩子送上船，带到他能找到的最荒凉、最可怕的地方，宝琳娜的丈夫虽极不情愿，但不得不这样做。

后来，可怜的王后因为更爱波力克希尼斯而不是国王而被判处叛国罪。但事实上，除了丈夫列昂特斯，她从来没有爱过别人。列昂特斯派使者叩求阿波罗神谕，询问他对王后的残忍想法是否正确。但是他没有耐心等待，他们回来时他已经在公开审判王后了。神谕称：

"赫美温妮清白无辜，波力克希尼斯无可指责，卡密罗忠心耿耿，列昂特斯善妒残暴。倘若国王不能改正错误，他将失去子嗣。"

随后，一个人来告诉他们，小王子死了。可怜的王后听到这话，一下子就晕倒了。这时，国王才明白他是多么邪恶和荒谬。他命令宝琳娜和侍女们把王后带走，让她苏醒过来。但宝琳娜一会儿就回来了，告诉国王赫美温妮死了。

现在，列昂特斯终于明白自己多么愚蠢了。王后死了，本来可以安慰他的小女儿被他送走了，成为狼和鸢的猎物。现在他已经一无所有了。他满心悲痛，在祈祷和悔恨中度过了许多悲伤的岁月。

小公主被留在波希米亚海岸，那属于波力克希尼斯的王国。宝琳娜的丈夫再也没有回家，没能告诉列昂特斯他把孩子留在了哪里；因为他返回船上时遇上了一头熊，被撕成碎片，丧了命。

但是这个被遗弃的可怜婴儿被一个牧羊人发现了。她穿着华丽的衣服，身边还放着珠宝，斗篷上别着一张纸条，上面写着她的名字叫帕笛塔，出身高贵。

牧羊人心地善良，把婴儿带回家交给妻子，他们把帕笛塔当作自己的孩子抚养成人。帕笛塔受过的教育并不比普通牧羊人家的孩子多，但她从母后那里继承了优雅和魅力，和她所居住村庄里的其他姑娘很不一样。

一天，贤明的波希米亚国王的儿子弗罗利泽王子在牧羊人的房子附近打猎，看见了帕笛塔，她现在长成了一个迷人的女子。他和牧羊人交上了朋友，但没有告诉牧羊人他是王子，而是说他叫托力格斯，是位深居简出的绅士。后来，他深深地爱上了美丽的帕笛塔，几乎每天都来看她。

国王不明白是什么原因让儿子几乎每天都离开家，于是派人监视他，结果发现波希米亚国王的继承人爱上了漂亮的牧羊女帕笛塔。波力克希尼斯想看看这是不是真的，就乔装改扮，和忠实的卡密罗一起去了老牧羊人的家。他们来到了剪羊毛的喜宴上，尽管他们是陌生人，却受到了热情的招待。舞会正在进行，一名小贩在卖丝带、花边和手套，都是年轻人买给他们情人的东西。

弗罗利泽和帕笛塔并没有加入这一欢乐的场面，而是安静地坐在一起聊天。国王注意到了帕笛塔优雅的举止和姣好的容貌，但从来没有想到帕笛塔是他的老朋友列昂特斯的女儿。他对卡密罗说：

"虽出身低贱，但她是这片草地上最美的贫家姑娘。她所做的一切或她的样子都显出一种比她自身更为高贵的品质——这个地方委屈了她。"

卡密罗回答说："千真万确，她就是这地方的女王。"

但弗罗利泽没认出他的父亲，还请陌生人见证他和漂亮的牧羊女订婚。国王公开了自己的身份，禁止这桩婚事，并补充说，如果牧羊女再见弗罗利泽的话，他将杀死牧羊女和她的老父亲——那个牧羊人。国王说完就离开了。但卡密罗留下来了，因为他被帕笛塔的魅力迷住了，想结识帕笛塔。

卡密罗早就知道列昂特斯对自己愚蠢的疯狂举动是多

么懊悔，他渴望回西西里去见他的旧主。现在他建议两个年轻人去列昂特斯那里寻求保护。于是他们去了，牧羊人也跟着去了，带着帕笛塔的珠宝、她的婴儿服，还有牧羊人在斗篷上找到的纸条。

列昂特斯热情地接待了他们。他对弗罗利泽王子很客气，但他的目光一直停留在帕笛塔身上。他看到帕笛塔那么像赫美温妮王后，一遍又一遍地说：

"如果我没有狠心地把女儿送走，她也会是这么可爱的人儿啊。"

老牧羊人听说国王失去了一个小女儿，她被留在波希米亚海岸上之后，他确信帕笛塔，他抚养长大的孩子，一定是国王的女儿。他讲述了他的故事，展示了珠宝和纸条后，国王确信帕笛塔是他失散已久的孩子。他高兴地欢迎帕笛塔，并报答了好心的牧羊人。

波力克希尼斯急忙追上他的儿子，阻止他和帕笛塔结婚，但当他发现帕笛塔是老朋友的女儿时，很高兴地同意了。

然而，列昂特斯并不高兴。他想起了美丽的王后，她本应该在他身边，分享女儿的幸福带来的喜悦，但王后因他不近人情而死去了，好长一段时间他只说了一句话：

"哦，你的母亲！你的母亲！"他请求波希米亚国王原谅他，接着亲吻了女儿和弗罗利泽王子，最后他感谢了老牧羊人的好心。

多年来，宝琳娜因为对赫美温妮王后很好，一直受到国王的青睐。她说："我为已故的王后制作了一尊雕像，耗时多年才完成，由意大利的旷世奇才朱利奥·罗马诺制作。我把它单独放在一所私宅里，自从您失去王后以来，我每天都过去两三趟。陛下愿意去看看雕像吗？"

于是，列昂特斯、波力克希尼斯、弗罗利泽和帕笛塔，连同卡密罗和他们的随从，都去了宝琳娜家，那里有一幅厚重的紫色帷幕遮住了一个凹室；宝琳娜把一只手放在帷幕上，说：

"她活着的时候是举世无双的，我确信她身后的雕像一定远胜你们所曾见到，或者人手所曾制作的一切。因此，我把它单独放在这里。它就在这儿——瞧瞧它，赞美它吧。"

说着，她拉开帷幕，让大家看那尊雕像。国王凝视着他去世妻子的美丽雕像，但什么也没说。

"我喜欢您的沉默，"宝琳娜说，"这说明您很惊奇。不过，您说，这不像她吗？"

"这几乎是她本人了，"国王说，"可是，宝琳娜，赫美温妮没有这么多皱纹，不像这座雕像一样老。"

"对，远不是这样老。"波力克希尼斯说。

"对，"宝琳娜说，"这是雕塑师的厉害之处，他向我们展示了王后如果活到现在会是什么样子。"

列昂特斯仍然望着雕像，无法把目光移开。

"如果我知道，"宝琳娜说，"这尊可怜的雕像会这样触动您的悲哀和爱意，我是不会给您看的。"

他只是回答说："不要拉上帷幕。"

"不，您不能再看了，"宝琳娜说，"否则您就要以为它是会动的了。"

"别动！别动！"国王说，"你不认为它在呼吸吗？"

"我要拉上帷幕了，"宝琳娜说，"否则您就要以为她是活的了。"

"啊，亲爱的宝琳娜，"列昂特斯说，"让我这么想下去，想二十年吧。"

"如果您还能承受，"宝琳娜说，"我可以叫这尊雕像动起来，走下来握住您的手。可是那时您一定会以为我施了妖法。"

"无论你能让她做什么，我都愿意看。"国王说。

在所有人的欣赏和注视下，雕像从底座上走下来，走下台阶，搂住国王的脖子，国王捧着她的脸庞，亲吻了好多次，因为这不是雕像，而是真正的、活着的赫美温妮王后本人。这些年来，她被善良的宝琳娜藏了起来，不让她的丈夫发现，尽管她知道丈夫已经悔过，但直到她知道了小女儿的下落，才完全原谅丈夫。

现在帕笛塔被找到了，她原谅了丈夫的一切过错。再次相聚，对他们来说就像一场新的、美好的婚姻。

弗罗利泽和帕笛塔结婚了，生活得长久而幸福。

对列昂特斯来说，在经历了漫长的悲伤和痛苦之后，在他再次被真爱拥抱的那一刻，多年的痛苦终于得到了补偿。

终成眷属

1300 年左右，罗西昂伯爵夫人在比利牛斯山附近的宫殿里过得很不愉快。她失去了丈夫，法兰西国王把她的儿子贝特兰召到了几百英里外的巴黎。

贝特兰是个漂亮的年轻人，长着拳曲的头发、精致的弯眉和敏锐如鹰的眼睛。他为无知感到骄傲，为自私的目的而撒谎。但是长得漂亮就足够了，海伦娜爱上了他。

海伦娜是一位已故名医的女儿，他曾为罗西昂伯爵效力。她唯一的财产就是父亲留下的一些处方。

贝特兰走后，海伦娜悲伤的神情引起了伯爵夫人的注意，她告诉海伦娜，对她来说，海伦娜就像自己的孩子一样。海伦娜的眼里噙满了泪水，因为她觉得伯爵夫人这么

ALL'S WELL THAT ENDS WELL.

一说，贝特兰成了一个她永远不能嫁的哥哥。伯爵夫人立即猜到了她的心思，海伦娜承认贝特兰对她来说就像太阳对白天一样重要。

她希望赢得法兰西国王的感激，从而赢得这个太阳。法兰西国王久病未愈，跛了脚。熟谙医术的御医们对治好他的病都已经束手无策，但海伦娜对她父亲成功使用过的处方充满信心。

她深情地向伯爵夫人告辞，去了巴黎，并获许觐见国王。

国王很有礼貌，但显然他认为海伦娜是个庸医。他说："那些医术高明的医生都不能医治好我，我决不会向一个无知的少女求医。"

海伦娜说："上天有时会借助弱者之手成事。"她说，如果她不能治好国王，国王可以处死她。

"如果你成功了呢？"国王问道。

"那么我就要请陛下把我选中之人赐给我做丈夫！"

一位受苦的国王无法始终拒绝一名如此真诚的年轻女子。海伦娜因此成为国王的医生，两天后，这位至尊的跛子竟可以蹦蹦跳跳了。

他召集了朝臣，他们如同群星令宫殿熠熠生辉。这位乡下姑娘看得眼花缭乱，在她面前的贵族中，有一大把值得托付终身的青年才俊。但她的目光一直在搜寻，直到找到贝特兰。随后，她走到贝特兰跟前说："我不敢说我选中了您，只能说我属于您了！"她提高声音，让国王听到，又补充说："这就是我选中的人！"

"贝特兰，"国王说，"你娶了她吧，她是你的妻子了！"

"我的妻子？"贝特兰说，"我请求陛下允许我为自己选择妻子。"

"贝特兰，你知道她为你的国王做了什么吗？"国王问，他把贝特兰当儿子看待。

"我知道，陛下，"贝特兰答道，"但我为什么要娶一个靠我父亲养活长大的姑娘呢？"

"你看不起她，是因为她没有头衔，但是我可以赐她头衔。"国王说。他望着这个闷闷不乐的年轻人，突然有了一个念头，他接着说："这真是一件怪事，倘若把你的血和乞丐的血盛在一个碗里，你自己都无法分辨它们，你居然还那么在乎血统。"

"我不能爱她。"贝特兰说。海伦娜温柔地说："陛下，请您不要逼他。我很高兴为我们国家治好了我的国王。"

"这事关我的荣誉，那小伙子必须服从我的旨意。"国王说，"贝特兰，下定决心吧。迎娶这位你配不上的女子，否则你就会见识国王的愤怒。你的答案是什么？"

贝特兰深深地鞠了一躬，说道："陛下已经使这位女子变得高贵了。我服从您。"

"牵着她的手，"国王说，"告诉她，她属于你了。"

贝特兰遵命行事，很快就和海伦娜结婚了。

然而，对国王的恐惧并不能使他成为一位爱人。嘲笑也使他不高兴。一个名叫帕洛的士兵当面告诉他，现在他有了一头"河东狮"，他的任务不是打仗，而是待在家里。贝特兰接受不了有这样一个妻子，他必须到意大利战场上去，尽管国王不准他去。

他命令海伦娜离开国王，回到罗西昂，并把写给母亲和海伦娜的信交给她。他冷淡地跟她告别，骑着马走了。

她打开那封写给她的信，念道："当你能从我手指上取走戒指时，你就可以叫我丈夫，但我敢打赌你永远也取不走。"

海伦娜同国王告别时没有哭，但国王为她感到不安，他从自己手指上取下一枚戒指给了她，说："如果你派人送来这枚戒指，我就知道你有麻烦了，我会帮助你。"

她没有给国王看贝特兰写给她的信。那会让国王生出杀死那个不负责任的伯爵的念头。她回到罗西昂，把另一封信交给婆婆。这是一封简短而苦涩的信。"我逃走了，"信上说，"如果世界足够宽广，我将永远远离她。"

"振作起来，"高贵的寡妇对弃妇说，"我和他断绝关系，你是我唯一的孩子。"

然而，老伯爵夫人仍然是贝特兰的母亲，并把他的错误归咎于帕洛，她称帕洛是"坏东西"。

海伦娜没有在罗西昂待多久。她乔装成一个朝圣者，给婆婆留下一封信，就偷偷地动身去佛罗伦萨了。

入城后，她问一个女人去朝圣者旅店的路，但是女人恳请这位"神圣的朝圣者"在她家寄宿。

海伦娜得知女房东是名寡妇，她有一个美丽的女儿叫狄安娜。

狄安娜听说海伦娜从法兰西来，便说："你的一个同胞，罗西昂伯爵，在佛罗伦萨立下很大的功劳。"但过了一会儿，狄安娜说出了一些与海伦娜的丈夫不般配的事情。贝特兰正向狄安娜大献殷勤。他没有隐瞒自己已婚的事实，狄安娜从帕洛那里听说他的妻子不足挂齿。

寡妇为狄安娜担忧，海伦娜决定告诉她，自己就是罗西昂伯爵夫人。

"他一直问狄安娜要一缕头发。"寡妇说。

海伦娜悲哀地笑了，因为她的头发和狄安娜的一样漂亮，颜色也一样。她想到了一个主意，说："您把这袋金子拿去。狄安娜若愿意帮我执行这个计划，我就给她三千克朗。让她答应，如果我丈夫把手指上戴的戒指给她，她就把她的一缕头发给我丈夫。那是先祖传下来的戒指，五位罗西昂伯爵都戴过，但他竟愿意用戒指换您女儿的一绺头发。让您女儿坚持要我丈夫在黑屋子里剪下她的一绺头发，让她同意事先一个字也不说。"

寡妇聚精会神地听着，膝头放着那袋金子。她终于说："我同意，只要狄安娜愿意。"

狄安娜很乐意，说来也奇怪，在一个黑暗的房间里从一个默不作声的姑娘头上割下一绺头发的想法，让贝特兰非常高兴，他同意把戒指送给狄安娜，而狄安娜告诉他什么时候跟着自己走进黑暗的房间。在约定的时间，他拿着一把锋利的刀来了，当他割下一绺头发时，感到一张甜美的脸碰到了他的脸，他满意地离开了房间，手指上戴着一枚戒指，那是姑娘在黑暗的房间里送给他的。

战争快结束了，在战事最后贝特兰才知道那个称海伦娜为"河东狮"的士兵远没有一位妻子勇敢。帕洛是一个骗子，他喜欢虚张声势，所以法兰西军官就跟他开了个玩笑，想看看他的为人。他的鼓丢了，他说过，除非他在战斗中牺牲，否则他一定会夺回鼓。他没有找回鼓，却编造了一个虽英勇战斗却遭遇失败，被包围缴械的故事。

"波托塔尔塔罗萨。"一名法兰西贵族说。

"这是什么意思？"帕洛想，他的眼睛被蒙上了。

"他要对你严刑拷打。"一个假装做翻译的法兰西人说，"你可以说些什么以免受皮肉之苦呢？"

"我可以告诉您很多秘密，"帕洛回答说，"就像您狠狠揍我一顿我能招的那么多。"他说到做到。他告诉他们佛罗伦萨军队每个团有多少人，还讲了一些指挥官们的逸事，给法兰西军官解乏。

贝特兰也在场，他听人读了一封信，帕洛在信中告诉狄安娜说贝特兰是个傻瓜。

"这就是您忠心的朋友。"一名法兰西贵族说。

"现在他在我眼中就是一只猫。"贝特兰说，他最讨厌的就是炉边地毯上的宠物。

帕洛终于被放了，但从那以后，他就活得鬼鬼祟祟，再也不敢到处吹嘘了。

我们现在跟着海伦娜回到法兰西，海伦娜散布了自己的死讯。拉佛把这个消息告诉了罗西昂伯爵夫人，他是一位贵族，想把自己的女儿穆德琳嫁给贝特兰。

国王为海伦娜哀悼，但他同意了贝特兰的婚事，并动身前往罗西昂以促成这桩婚事。

"他所犯的重大过失已经过去了，"他说，"让贝特兰过来见我吧。"

脸颊上伤痕累累的贝特兰跪在君主面前说，如果他在娶海伦娜之前没有爱上拉佛的女儿，他就会珍惜妻子，现在爱海伦娜却为时已晚。

"迟来的爱令那伟大的发送者愤怒。"国王说，"忘记可爱的海伦娜，把你的戒指送给穆德琳吧。"

贝特兰立刻把戒指给了拉佛，拉佛生气地说："这是海伦娜的！"

"这不是她的！"贝特兰说。

国王看着戒指说："这是我送给海伦娜的戒指，让她在需要帮助时派人送给我。所以是你用诡计从她那里夺走了最能帮助她的东西。"

贝特兰再次否认戒指是海伦娜的，可就连他的母亲也说是她的。

"你撒谎！"国王叫道，"把他拿下，卫兵！"但就在他们抓住他的时候，贝特兰还在想，他以为是狄安娜送给他的那枚戒指怎么会跟海伦娜的戒指那么像？这时一位绅士走进来，递给国王一封信。信署名狄安娜·卡必莱特，信上央求国王下令让贝特兰娶她，因为贝特兰在赢得她的爱后抛弃了她。

"现在我宁可在集市上买一个女婿，也好过让贝特兰做我的女婿。"拉佛说。

"把狄安娜带进来。"国王说。

贝特兰与狄安娜及她的母亲当面对质。他否认狄安娜和他有任何关系，谈起狄安娜就好像狄安娜是在阴沟里生活的。但是狄安娜问他为什么要把先祖的戒指送给这样一个姑娘，现在他手指上的戒指已经不见。

贝特兰羞愧得无地自容，但命运对他非常慷慨。海伦娜走了进来。

"我看见的是真的吗？"国王问。

"啊，原谅我！原谅我！"贝特兰大喊道。

海伦娜拿起他先祖的戒指。"现在我有这个，"她说，"贝特兰，你会爱我吗？"

"至死不渝。"他喊道。

"我的眼睛像被洋葱熏到了。"拉佛说，眼中闪烁着要为海伦娜流下的泪水。

国王从这位不太害羞的年轻女士那里充分了解到她行为的用意后，赞扬了狄安娜。为了海伦娜，她希望不仅在国王面前，而且在贝特兰自己面前揭露贝特兰的卑鄙行径。他的骄傲现在已荡然无存，人们相信他终究还是成了一位丈夫。

CONTENTS

A MIDSUMMER NIGHT'S DREAM

Hermia and Lysander were lovers; but Hermia's father wished her to marry another man, named Demetrius.

Now, in Athens, where they lived, there was a wicked law, by which any girl who refused to marry according to her father's wishes, might be put to death. Hermia's father was so angry with her for refusing to do as he wished, that he actually brought her before the Duke of Athens to ask that she might be killed, if she still refused to obey him. The Duke gave her four days to think about it, and, at the end of that time, if she still refused to marry Demetrius, she would have to die.

Lysander of course was nearly mad with grief, and the best thing he thought Hermia should do is to run away to his aunt's house at a place beyond the reach of that cruel law; and there he would come to her and marry her. But before she started, she told her friend, Helena, what she was going to do.

Helena had been Demetrius' sweetheart long before his marriage with Hermia had been thought of, and being very silly, like all jealous people, she could not see that it was not poor Hermia's fault that Demetrius wished to marry her instead of his own lady, Helena. She knew that if she told Demetrius that Hermia was going to the wood outside Athens, he would follow her, "and I can follow him, and at least I shall see him," she said to herself. So she went to him, and betrayed her friend's secret.

Now this wood where Lysander was to meet Hermia, and where the other two had decided to follow them, was full of fairies, as most woods are; in this wood on this night were the King and Queen of the fairies, Oberon and Titania. Fairies are very wise people, but now and then they can be quite as foolish as human beings. Oberon and Titania, who might have been as happy as the days were long, had thrown away all their joy in a foolish quarrel. They never met without saying disagreeable things to each other, and scolded each other so dreadfully that all their little fairy followers, for fear, would creep into acorn cups and hide there.

So, instead of keeping one happy Court and dancing all night through in the moonlight, the King with his attendants wandered through one part of the wood, while the Queen with hers in another. And the cause of all this trouble was a little Indian boy whom Titania had taken to be one of her followers. Oberon wanted the child to follow him and be one of his fairy knights; but the Queen would not give him up.

On this night, in a mossy moonlit glade, the King and Queen of the fairies met.

"Ill met by moonlight, proud Titania," said the King.

"What? jealous, Oberon!" answered the Queen.

"You spoil everything with your quarreling. Come, fairies, let us leave him. I am not friends with him now."

"It is you who make up the quarrel," said the King.

"Give me that little Indian boy, and I will again be your humble servant and suitor."

"Set your mind at rest," said the Queen. "Your whole fairy kingdom cannot buy that boy from me. Come, fairies."

And she and her train rode off down the moonbeams.

"Well, go your ways," said Oberon. "But I'll be even with you before you leave this wood."

Then Oberon called his favorite fairy, Puck. Puck was the spirit of mischief. He used to slip into the dairies and take the cream away, and get into the churn so that the butter would not come, and turn the beer sour, and lead people out of their way on dark nights and then laugh at them, and tumble people's stools from under them when they were going to sit down, and upset their hot ale over their chins when they were going to drink.

"Now," said Oberon to this little sprite, "fetch me the flower called Love-in-idleness. The juice of that little purple flower laid on the eyes of those who sleep will make them, when they wake, to love the first thing they see. I will put some of the juice of that flower on my Titania's eyes, and when she wakes she will love the first thing she sees, were it a lion, bear, or wolf, or bull, or a meddling monkey, or a busy ape."

While Puck was gone, Demetrius passed through the glade followed by poor Helena, and still she told him how she loved him and reminded him of all his promises, and still he told her that he did not and could not love her, and that his promises were nothing. Oberon was sorry for poor Helena, and when Puck returned with the flower, he ordered him to follow Demetrius and put some of the juice on his eyes, so that he might love Helena when he woke and looked on her, as much as she loved him. So Puck set off, and wandering through the wood found, not Demetrius, but Lysander, on whose eyes he put the juice; but when Lysander woke, he saw not his own Hermia, but Helena, who was walking through the wood looking for the cruel Demetrius; and when he saw her, he directly loved her and left his own lady, under the spell of the purple flower.

When Hermia woke she found Lysander gone, and wandered about the wood trying to find him. Puck went back and told Oberon what he had done, and Oberon soon found that he had made a mistake, and set about looking for Demetrius, and having found him, put some of the juice on his eyes. And the first thing Demetrius saw when he woke was also Helena. So now Demetrius and Lysander were both following her through the wood, and it was Hermia's turn to follow her lover as Helena had done before. The end of it was that Helena and Hermia began to quarrel, and Demetrius and Lysander went off to fight. Oberon was very sorry to see his kind scheme to help these lovers turn out so badly. So he said to Puck—

"These two young men are going to fight. You must cover the night with drooping fog, and lead them so astray, that one will never find the other. When they are tired out, they will fall asleep. Then drop this other herb on Lysander's eyes. That will give him his old sight and his old love. Then each man will have the lady who loves him, and they will all think that this has been only a Midsummer Night's Dream. Then when this is done, all will be well with them."

So Puck went and did as he was told, and when the two had fallen asleep without meeting each other, Puck poured the juice on Lysander's eyes, and said—

"When you wake,

You take

True delight

In the sight

Of your former lady's eye:

Jack shall have Jill;

Nothing shall go ill."

Meanwhile Oberon found Titania asleep on a bank where grew all kinds of flowers. There Titania always slept a part of the night, wrapped in the skin of a snake. Oberon stooped over her and laid the juice on her eyes, saying—

"What you see when you wake,

Do it for your true love take."

Now, it happened that when Titania woke the first thing she saw was a stupid clown, one of a party of players who had come out into the wood to rehearse their play. This clown had met with Puck, who had clapped an ass's head on his shoulders so that it looked as if it grew there. Directly Titania woke and saw this dreadful monster, she said, "What angel is this? Are you as wise as you are beautiful?"

"If I am wise enough to find my way out of this wood, that's enough for me," said the foolish clown.

"Do not desire to go out of the wood," said Titania. The spell of the love-juice was on her, and to her the clown seemed the most beautiful and delightful creature on all the earth. "I love you," she went on. "Come with me, and I will give you fairies to attend on you."

So she called four fairies, whose names were Peaseblossom, Cobweb, Moth, and Mustardseed.

"You must attend this gentleman," said the Queen. "Feed him with apricots and dewberries, purple grapes, green figs, and mulberries. Steal honey-bags for him from the bumble-bees, and with the wings of painted butterflies fan the moonbeams from his sleeping eyes."

"I will," said one of the fairies, and all the others said, "I will."

"Now, sit down with me," said the Queen to the clown, "and let me stroke your dear cheeks, and stick musk-roses in your smooth, sleek head, and kiss your fair large ears, my gentle joy."

"Where's Peaseblossom?" asked the clown with the ass's head. He did not care much about the Queen's affection, but he was very proud of having fairies to wait on him. "Ready," said Peaseblossom.

"Scratch my head, Peaseblossom," said the clown. "Where's Cobweb?" "Ready," said Cobweb.

"Kill me," said the clown, "the red bumble-bee on the top of the thistle yonder, and bring me the honey-bag. Where's Mustardseed?" "Ready," said Mustardseed.

"Oh, I want nothing," said the clown. "Only just help Cobweb to scratch. I must go to the barber's, for I think my face is extremely hairy."

"Would you like anything to eat?" said the fairy Queen.

"I should like some good dry oats," said the clown—for his donkey's head made him desire donkey's food—"and some hay to follow."

"Shall some of my fairies fetch you new nuts from the squirrel's house?" asked the Queen.

"I'd rather have a handful or two of good dried peas," said the clown. "But please don't let any of your people disturb me; I am going to sleep."

Then said the Queen, "And I will hold you in my arms."

And so when Oberon came along he found his beautiful Queen kissing a clown with a donkey's head.

And before he released her from the enchantment, he persuaded her to give him the little Indian boy he so much desired to have. Then he took pity on her, and threw some juice of the disenchanting flower on her pretty eyes; and then in a moment she saw plainly the donkey-headed clown she had been loving, and knew how foolish she had been.

Oberon took off the ass's head from the clown, and left him to finish his sleep with his own silly head lying on the flowers.

Thus all was made plain and straight again. Oberon and Titania loved each other more than ever. Demetrius thought of no one but Helena, and Helena had never had any thought of anyone but Demetrius.

As for Hermia and Lysander, they were the most loving couple you could meet, even through a fairy wood.

So the four mortal lovers went back to Athens and were married; and the fairy King and Queen live happily together in that very wood at this very day.

THE MERCHANT
OF VENICE

Antonio was a rich and prosperous merchant of Venice. His ships were on nearly every sea, and he traded with Portugal, with Mexico, with England, and with India. Although proud of his riches, he was very generous with them, and delighted to use them in relieving the wants of his friends, among whom his relation, Bassanio, held the first place.

Now Bassanio, like many another gay and gallant gentleman, was reckless and extravagant, and finding that he had not only come to the end of his fortune, but was also unable to pay his creditors, he went to Antonio for further help.

"To you, Antonio," he said, "I owe the most in money and in love: and I have thought of a plan to pay everything I owe if you will but help me."

"Say what I can do, and it shall be done," answered his friend.

Then said Bassanio, "In Belmont there is a rich lady, and from all quarters of the globe renowned suitors come to woo her, not only because she is rich, but because she is beautiful and good as well. She looked on me with such favor when last we met, that I feel sure that I should win her away from all rivals for her love had I but the means to go to Belmont, where she lives."

"All my fortunes," said Antonio, "are at sea, and so I have no ready money; but luckily my credit is good in Venice, and I will borrow for you what you need."

There was living in Venice at this time a rich money-lender, named Shylock. Antonio despised and disliked this man very much, and treated him with the greatest harshness and scorn. He would thrust him over his threshold, and would even spit on him. Shylock submitted to all these indignities with a patient shrug; but deep in his heart he cherished a desire for revenge on the rich, smug merchant. "I should be richer than Antonio by half a million ducats. On the market place, and wherever he can, he denounces the rate of interest I charge, and—worse than that—he lends out money freely."

So when Bassanio came to him to ask for a loan of three thousand ducats to Antonio for three months, Shylock hid his hatred, and turning to Antonio, said—"Harshly as you have treated me, I would be friends with you and have your love. So I will lend you the money and charge you no interest. But, just for fun, you shall sign a bond in which it shall be agreed that if you do not repay me in three months' time, then I shall have the right to a pound of your flesh, to be cut from what part of your body I choose."

"No," cried Bassanio to his friend, "you shall run no such risk for me."

"Why, fear not," said Antonio, "my ships will be home a month before the time. I will sign the bond."

Thus Bassanio can go to Belmont, there to woo

the lovely Portia. The very night he started, the money-lender's pretty daughter, Jessica, ran away from her father's house with her lover, and she took with her from her father's hoards some bags of ducats and precious stones. Shylock's grief and anger were terrible to see. His love for her changed to hate. "I would she were dead at my feet and the jewels in her ear," he cried. His only comfort now was in hearing of the serious losses which had befallen Antonio, some of whose ships were wrecked. "Let him look to his bond," said Shylock, "let him look to his bond."

Meanwhile Bassanio had reached Belmont, and had visited the fair Portia. He found, as he had told Antonio, that the rumor of her wealth and beauty had drawn to her suitors from far and near. But to all of them Portia had but one reply. She would only accept that suitor who would pledge himself to abide by the terms of her father's will. These were conditions that frightened away many an ardent suiter. For he who would win Portia's heart and hand, had to guess which of the three caskets held her portrait. If he guessed it right, then Portia would be his bride; if wrong, then he was bound by oath never to reveal which casket he chose, never to marry, and to go away at once.

The caskets were of gold, silver, and lead. The gold one bore this inscription:"Who chooses me shall gain what many men desire;" the silver one had this:"Who chooses me shall get as much as he deserves;" while on the lead one were these words:"Who chooses me must give and run the risk of losing all he has." The Prince of Morocco, as brave as he was black, was among the first to submit to this test. He chose the gold casket, for he said neither lead nor silver could contain her picture. He found inside the likeness of what many men desire—death.

After him came the pride Prince of Arragon, and saying, "Let me have what I deserve—surely I deserve the lady," he chose the silver one, and found inside a fool's head. "Did I deserve no more than a fool's head?" he cried.

Then at last came Bassanio, and Portia would have delayed him from making his choice from very fear of his choosing wrong. For she loved him dearly, even as he loved her. "But," said Bassanio, "let me choose at once, for, as I am, I live upon the rack."

Then Portia bade her servants to bring music and play while her brave lover made his choice. And Bassanio took the oath and walked up to the caskets, while the musicians playing softly. "Mere outward show," he said, "is to be despised. The world is still deceived with ornament, and so no gaudy gold or shining silver for me. I choose the lead casket; joy be the consequence!" And opening it, he found fair Portia's portrait inside, and he turned to her and asked if it were true that she was his.

"Yes," said Portia, "I am yours, and this house is yours, and with them I give you this ring, from which you must never part."

And Bassanio, saying that he could hardly speak for joy, found words to swear that he would never part with the ring while he lived.

Then suddenly all his happiness was dashed with sorrow, for messengers came from Venice to tell him that Antonio was ruined, and that Shylock demanded from the Duke the fulfilment of the bond, under which he was entitled to a pound of the merchant's flesh. Portia was as grieved as Bassanio to hear of the danger which threatened his friend.

"First," she said, "take me to church and make me your wife, and then go to Venice at once to help your friend. You shall take with you money enough to pay his debt twenty times over."

But when her newly-made husband had gone, Portia went after him, and arrived in Venice disguised as a lawyer, and with an introduction from a celebrated lawyer Bellario, whom the Duke of Venice had called in to decide the legal questions raised by Shylock's claim to a pound of Antonio's flesh. When the Court met, Bassanio offered Shylock twice the money borrowed, if he would withdraw his claim. But the money-lender's only answer was—

"If every ducat in six thousand ducats,

Were in six parts, and every part a ducat,

I would not draw them—I would have my bond."

It was then that Portia arrived in her disguise, and not even her own husband knew her. The Duke gave her welcome on account of the great Bellario's introduction, and left the settlement of the case to her. Then in noble words she bade Shylock have mercy. But he was deaf to her entreaties.

"I will have the pound of flesh," was his reply.

"What have you to say?" asked Portia of the merchant.

"But little," he answered, "I am well prepared."

"The Court awards you a pound of Antonio's flesh," said Portia to the money-lender.

"Most righteous judge!" cried Shylock. "A sentence: come, prepare."

"Wait a minute. This bond gives you no right to Antonio's blood, only to his flesh. If, then, you spill a drop of his blood, all your property will be forfeited to the State. Such is the Law."

And Shylock, in his fear, said, "Then I will take Bassanio's offer."

"No," said Portia sternly, "you shall have nothing but your bond. Take your pound of flesh, but remember, that if you take more or less, even by the weight of a hair, you will lose your property and your life."

Shylock now grew very much frightened. "Give me my three thousand ducats that I lent him, and let him go."

Bassanio would have paid it to him, but said Portia, "No! He shall have nothing but his bond."

"You, a foreigner," she added, "have sought to take the life of a Venetian citizen, and thus by the Venetian law, your life and goods are forfeited. Down, therefore, and beg mercy of the Duke."

Thus were the tables turned, and no mercy would have been shown to Shylock had it not been for Antonio. As it was, the money-lender forfeited half his fortune to the State, and he had to settle the other half on his daughter's husband, and with this he had to be content.

Bassanio, in his gratitude to the clever lawyer, was induced to part with the ring his wife had given him, and with which he had promised never to part, and when on his return to Belmont he confessed as much to Portia, she seemed very angry, and vowed she would not be friends with him until she had her ring again. But at last she told him that it was she who, in the disguise of the lawyer, had saved his friend's life, and got the ring from him. So Bassanio was forgiven, and made happier than ever, to know how rich a prize he had drawn in the lottery of the caskets.

TWELFTH NIGHT

Orsino, the Duke of Illyria, was deeply in love with a beautiful Countess named Olivia. Yet was all his love in vain, for she disdained his suit; and when her brother died, she sent back a messenger from the Duke, bidding him tell his master that for seven years she would not let the very air see her face, but that, like a nun, she would walk veiled; and all this for the sake of a dead brother's love, which she would keep fresh and lasting in her sad remembrance.

The Duke longed for someone to whom he could tell his sorrow, and repeat over and over again the story of his love. And chance brought him such a companion. For about this time a ship was wrecked on the Illyrian coast, and among those who reached land in safety were the captain and a fair young maid, named Viola. But she was little grateful for being rescued from the perils of the sea, since she feared that her twin brother was drowned, Sebastian, as dear to her as the heart in her bosom, and so like her that, but for the difference in their manner of dress, one could hardly be told from the other. The captain, for her comfort, told her that he had seen her brother bind himself "to a strong mast that lived upon the sea," and that thus there was hope that he might be saved.

Viola now asked in whose country she was, and learning that the young Duke Orsino ruled there, and was as noble in his nature as in his name, she decided to disguise herself as a man, and try to be employed as his servant.

In this she succeeded, and now from day to day she had to listen to the story of Orsino's love. At first she sympathized very truly with him, but soon her sympathy grew to love. At last it occurred to Orsino that his hopeless love-suit might prosper better if he sent this pretty lad to talk with Olivia for him. Viola unwillingly went on this errand, but when she came to the house, Malvolio, Olivia's steward, a vain, officious man, sick of self-love, did not let him in.

Viola, however (who was now called Cesario), refused to take any denial, and vowed to have speech with the Countess. Olivia, hearing how her instructions were defied and curious to see this daring youth, said, "We'll once more hear Orsino's embassy."

When Viola was admitted to her presence and the servants had been sent away, she listened patiently to the reproaches which this bold messenger from the Duke poured upon her, and she fell in love with the supposed Cesario; and when Cesario had gone, Olivia longed to send some gift to him. So, calling Malvolio, she ordered him to follow the boy.

"He left this ring behind him," she said, taking one from her finger. "Tell him I will not have it."

Malvolio did as he was ordered, and then Viola, who of course knew perfectly well that she had left no ring behind her, saw with a woman's quickness that Olivia loved her. Then she went back to the

Duke, very sad at heart for her lover, and for Olivia, and for herself.

It was but cold comfort she could give Orsino, who now sought to ease the hurt of despised love by listening to sweet music, while Cesario stood by his side.

"Ah," said the Duke to his servant that night, "you too have been in love."

"A little," answered Viola.

"What kind of woman is it?" he asked.

"Of your complexion," she answered.

"What years?" was his next question.

To this came the pretty answer, "About your years, my lord."

"Too old, by Heaven!" cried the Duke. "Let still the woman take an elder than herself."

And Viola very meekly said, "I think it well, my lord."

By and by Orsino begged Cesario once more to visit Olivia and to plead his love-suit. But she, thinking to dissuade him, said—

"If some lady loved you as you love Olivia?"

"Ah! that cannot be," said the Duke.

"But I know," Viola went on, "what love woman may have for a man. My father had a daughter loved a man, as it might be," she added blushing, "perhaps, were I a woman, I should love your lordship."

"And what is her history?" he asked.

"A blank, my lord," Viola answered. "She never told her love, but let concealment like a worm in the bud feed on her rosy cheek: she pined in thought, and sat there smiling sadly. Was not this love indeed?"

"But did your sister die of her love, my boy?" the Duke asked; and Viola, who had all the time been telling her own love for him in this pretty fashion, said—

"I am all the daughters my father has and all the brothers— Sir, shall I go to the lady?"

"To her in haste," said the Duke, at once forgetting all about the story, "and give her this jewel."

So Viola went, and this time poor Olivia was unable to hide her love, and openly confessed it with such passionate truth, that Viola left her hastily, saying—

"I will say no more words for my master."

But in vowing this, Viola did not know the tender pity she would feel for other's suffering. So when Olivia, in the violence of her love, sent a messenger, praying Cesario to visit her once more, Cesario had no heart to refuse the request.

But the favors which Olivia showed to this servant aroused the jealousy of Sir Andrew Aguecheek, a foolish, rejected lover of hers, who at that time was staying at her house with her merry old uncle Sir Toby. This same Sir Toby dearly loved a practical joke, and knowing Sir Andrew to be a total coward, he thought he could bring off a duel between him and Cesario. So he induced Sir Andrew to send a challenge, which he himself took to Cesario. The poor servant, in great terror, said—

"I will return again to the house, I am no fighter."

"Back you shall not to the house," said Sir Toby, "unless you fight me first."

And as he looked a very fierce old gentleman, Viola thought it best to await Sir Andrew's coming; and when he at last made his appearance, in a great fright, if the truth had been known, she tremblingly drew her sword, and Sir Andrew with fear followed her example. Happily for them both, at this moment some officers of the Court came on the scene, and stopped the intended duel. Viola gladly went away at once, while Sir Toby called after her—

"You are a coward!"

Now, while these things were happening, Sebastian had escaped all the dangers, and had landed safely in Illyria, where he determined to make his way to the Duke's Court. On his way he passed Olivia's house just as Viola had left it in such a hurry, and he met only Sir Andrew and Sir Toby. Sir Andrew, mistaking Sebastian for the cowardly Cesario, took his courage, walking up to him and struck him, saying, "There's for you."

"Why, there's for you; and there, and there!" said Sebastian, bitting back a great deal harder, and again and again, till Sir Toby came to the rescue of his friend. Sebastian, however, tore himself free from Sir Toby's clutches, and drawing his sword would have fought them both, but that Olivia herself, having heard of the quarrel, came running in, and with many reproaches sent Sir Toby and his friend away. Then turning to

Sebastian, whom she too thought to be Cesario, she asked him to come into the house with her.

Sebastian, half dazed and all delighted with her beauty and grace, readily consented, and that very day they were married before Olivia had discovered that he was not Cesario, or Sebastian was quite certain whether or not he was in a dream.

Meanwhile Orsino, hearing how ill Cesario sped with Olivia, visited her himself, taking Cesario with him. Olivia met them both before her door, and seeing, as she thought, her husband there, reproached him for leaving her, while to the Duke she said that his suit was disgusting.

"Still so cruel?" said Orsino.

"Still so constant," she answered.

Then Orsino's anger growing to cruelty, he vowed that, to be revenged on her, he would kill Cesario, whom he knew she loved. "Come, boy," he said to the servant.

And Viola, following him as he moved away, said, "I, to do you rest, a thousand deaths would die."

A great fear took hold on Olivia, and she cried

aloud, "Cesario, husband, stay!"

"Her husband?" asked the Duke angrily.

"No, my lord, not I," said Viola.

"Call forth the holy father," cried Olivia.

And the priest who had married Sebastian and Olivia, coming in, declared Cesario to be the bridegroom.

"O you are a liar!" the Duke exclaimed. "Farewell, and take her, but go where you and I henceforth may never meet again."

At this moment Sir Andrew came up with bleeding head, complaining that Cesario had broken his head, and Sir Toby's as well.

"I never hurt you," said Viola, very firmly, "you drew your sword on me, but I went away, and hurt you not."

Yet, for all her protesting, no one there believed her; but all their thoughts were on a sudden changed to wonder, when Sebastian came in.

"I am sorry, madam," he said to his wife, "I have hurt your kinsman. Pardon me, sweet, even for the vows we made to each other so late ago."

"One face, one voice, one habit, and two persons!" cried the Duke, looking first at Viola, and then at Sebastian.

"An apple cut in two," said one who knew Sebastian, "is not more twin than these two men. Which is Sebastian?"

"I never had a brother," said Sebastian. "I had a sister, whom the blind waves and surges have devoured." "Were you a woman," he said to Viola, "I should let my tears fall upon your cheek, and say, 'Welcome, drowned Viola!'"

Then Viola, happy to see her dear brother alive, confessed that she was indeed his sister, Viola. As she spoke, Orsino felt the pity that is similar to love.

"Boy," he said, "you have said to me a thousand times that you love a lady like me."

"I swear all those sayings are true," Viola replied.

"Give me your hand," Orsino cried in gladness. "You shall be my wife, and my fancy's queen."

Thus was the gentle Viola made happy, while Olivia found in Sebastian a constant lover, and a good husband, and he in her a true and loving wife.

AS YOU LIKE IT

There was once a wicked Duke named Frederick, who took the dukedom that should have belonged to his brother, sending him into exile. His brother went into the Forest of Arden, where he lived the life of a bold forester, as Robin Hood did in Sherwood Forest in merry England.

The banished Duke's daughter, Rosalind, remained with Celia, Frederick's daughter, and the two loved each other more than most sisters. One day there was a wrestling match at Court, and Rosalind and Celia went to see it. Charles, a celebrated wrestler, was there, who had killed many men in contests of this kind. Orlando, the young man he was to wrestle with, was so slender and youthful, that Rosalind and Celia thought he would surely be killed, as others had been; so they spoke to him, and asked him not to attempt so dangerous an adventure; but the only effect of their words was to make him wish more to come off well in the encounter, so as to win praise from such sweet ladies.

Orlando, like Rosalind's father, was being kept out of his inheritance by his brother, and was so sad at his brother's unkindness that, until he saw Rosalind, he did not care much whether he lived or died. But now the sight of the fair Rosalind gave him strength and courage, so that he did marvelously, and at last, threw Charles so badly. Duke Frederick was pleased with his courage, and asked his name.

"My name is Orlando, and I am the youngest son of Sir Rowland de Boys," said the young man.

Now Sir Rowland de Boys, when he was alive, had been a good friend to the banished Duke, so that Frederick heard with regret whose son Orlando was, and would not befriend him. But Rosalind was delighted to hear that this handsome young stranger was the son of her father's old friend, and as they were going away, she turned back more than once to say another kind word to the brave young man.

"Gentleman," she said, giving him a chain from her neck, "wear this for me."

Rosalind and Celia, when they were alone, began to talk about the handsome wrestler, and Rosalind confessed that she loved him at first sight.

"Come, come," said Celia, "wrestle with your affections."

"Oh," answered Rosalind, "they take the part of a better wrestler than myself. Look, here comes the Duke."

"With his eyes full of anger," said Celia.

"You must leave the Court at once," he said to Rosalind.

"Why?" she asked.

"Never mind why," answered the Duke, "you are banished. If within ten days you are found within twenty miles of my Court, you die."

So Rosalind set out to seek her father, the banished

Duke, in the Forest of Arden. Celia loved her too much to let her go alone. As it was rather a dangerous journey, Rosalind, being the taller, dressed up as a young countryman, and her cousin as a country girl, and Rosalind said that she would be called Ganymede, and Celia, Aliena. They were very tired when at last they came to the Forest of Arden, and as they were sitting on the grass a countryman passed that way, and Ganymede asked him if he could get them food. He did so, and told them that a shepherd's flocks and house were to be sold. They bought these and settled down as shepherd and shepherdess in the forest.

In the meantime, Oliver having sought to take his brother Orlando's life, Orlando also wandered into the forest, and there met with the rightful Duke, and being kindly received, stayed with him. Now, Orlando could think of nothing but Rosalind, and he went about the forest carving her name on trees, and writing love sonnets and hanging them on the bushes, and there Rosalind and Celia found them. One day Orlando met them, but he did not know Rosalind in her boy's clothes, though he liked the pretty shepherd youth, because he fancied a likeness in him to her.

"There is a foolish lover," said Rosalind, "who haunts these woods and hangs sonnets on the trees. If I could find him, I would soon cure him of his folly."

Orlando confessed that he was the foolish lover, and Rosalind said—"If you will come and see me every day, I will pretend to be Rosalind, and I will take her part, and be wayward and contrary, as is the way of women, till I make you ashamed of your folly in loving her."

And so every day he went to her house, and took a pleasure in saying to her all the pretty things he would have said to Rosalind; and she had the fine and secret joy of knowing that all his love-words came to the right ears. Thus many days passed pleasantly away.

One morning, as Orlando was going to visit Ganymede, he saw a man asleep on the ground, and that there was a lioness crouching near, waiting for the man who was asleep to wake: for they say that lions will not prey on anything that is dead or sleeping. Then Orlando looked at the man, and saw that it was his wicked brother, Oliver, who had tried to take his life. He fought with the lioness and killed her, and saved his brother's life.

While Orlando was fighting the lioness, Oliver woke to see his brother, whom he had treated so badly, saving him from a wild beast at the risk of his own life. This made him repent of his wickedness, and he begged Orlando's pardon, and from then on they were dear brothers. The lioness had wounded Orlando's arm so much, that he could not go on to see the shepherd, so he sent his brother to ask Ganymede to come to him.

Oliver went and told the whole story to Ganymede and Aliena, and Aliena was so charmed with his manly way of confessing his faults, that she fell in love with him at once. But when Ganymede heard of the danger Orlando had been in she fainted; and when she came to herself, she said truly enough, "I should have been a woman by right."

Oliver went back to his brother and told him all

this, saying, "I love Aliena so well that I will give up my estates to you and marry her, and live here as a shepherd."

"Let your wedding be tomorrow," said Orlando, "and I will ask the Duke and his friends."

When Orlando told Ganymede how his brother was to be married the next day, he added: "Oh, how bitter a thing it is to look into happiness through another man's eyes."

Then answered Rosalind, still in Ganymede's dress and speaking with his voice—"If you do love Rosalind so near the heart, then when your brother marries Aliena, shall you marry her."

Now the next day the Duke and his followers, and Orlando, and Oliver, and Aliena, were all gathered together for the wedding.

Then Ganymede came in and said to the Duke, "If I bring in your daughter Rosalind, will you give her to Orlando here?" "That I would," said the Duke, "if I had all kingdoms to give her with."

"And you say you will have her when I bring her?" she said to Orlando. "That would I," he answered, "were I king of all kingdoms."

Then Rosalind and Celia went out, and Rosalind put on her pretty woman's clothes again, and after a while came back.

She turned to her father, "I give myself to you, for I am yours." "If there be truth in sight," he said, "you are my daughter."

Then she said to Orlando, "I give myself to you, for I am yours." "If there be truth in sight," he said, "you are my Rosalind."

"I will have no father if you be not he," she said to the Duke, and to Orlando, "I will have no husband if you be not he."

So Orlando and Rosalind were married, and Oliver and Celia, and they lived happily ever after, returning with the Duke to the kingdom. For Frederick had been shown by a holy hermit the wickedness of his ways, and so gave back the dukedom to his brother, and himself went into a monastery to pray for forgiveness.

The wedding was a merry one, in the mossy glades of the forest. A shepherd and shepherdess who had been friends with Rosalind, when she was herself disguised as a shepherd, were married on the same day, and all with such pretty feastings and merrymakings as could be in no rooms, but only in the beautiful green wood.

MUCH ADO ABOUT NOTHING

❦

In Sicily is a town called Messina, which is the scene of a curious storm in a teacup that raged several hundred years ago.

It began with sunshine. Don Pedro, Prince of Arragon, in Spain, had gained so complete a victory over his foes that the very land whence they came is forgotten. Feeling happy and playful after the fatigues of war, Don Pedro came for a holiday to Messina, and in his suite were his stepbrother Don John and two young Italian lords, Benedick and Claudio.

Benedick was a merry chatterbox, who had determined to live a bachelor. Claudio, on the other hand, no sooner arrived at Messina than he fell in love with Hero, the daughter of Leonato, Governor of Messina.

One July day, a perfumer called Borachio was burning dried lavender in a musty room in Leonato's house, when the sound of conversation floated through the open window.

"Give me your candid opinion of Hero," Claudio asked, and Borachio settled himself for comfortable listening.

"Too short and brown for praise," was Benedick's reply, "but alter her color or height, and you spoil her."

"In my eyes she is the sweetest of women," said Claudio.

"Not in mine," retorted Benedick, "and I have no need for glasses. She is like the last day of December compared with the first of May if you set her beside her cousin. Unfortunately, Lady Beatrice is a fury."

Beatrice was Leonato's niece. She amused herself by saying witty and severe things about Benedick, who called her Dear Lady Disdain. She was wont to say that she was born under a dancing star, and could not therefore be dull.

Claudio and Benedick were still talking when Don Pedro came up and said good-humoredly, "Well, gentlemen, what's the secret?"

"I am longing," answered Benedick, "for your Grace to command me to tell."

"I charge you, then, to tell me honestly," said Don Pedro, falling in with his humor.

"I can be as dumb as a mute," apologized Benedick to Claudio, "but his Grace commands my speech." To Don Pedro he said, "Claudio is in love with Hero, Leonato's short daughter."

Don Pedro was pleased, for he admired Hero and was fond of Claudio. When Benedick had departed, he said to Claudio, "Be steadfast in your love for Hero, and I will help you to win her. Tonight her father gives a masquerade, and I will pretend I am Claudio, and tell her how Claudio loves her, and if she be pleased, I will go to her father and ask his consent to your union."

Most men like to do their own wooing, but if you

fall in love with a Governor's only daughter, you are fortunate if you can trust a Prince to plead for you.

Claudio then was fortunate, but he was unfortunate as well, for he had an enemy who was outwardly a friend. This enemy was Don Pedro's stepbrother Don John, who was jealous of Claudio because Don Pedro preferred him to Don John.

It was to Don John that Borachio came with the interesting conversation which he had overheard.

"I shall have some fun at that masquerade myself," said Don John when Borachio ceased speaking.

On the night of the masquerade, Don Pedro, masked and pretending he was Claudio, asked Hero if he might walk with her.

They moved away together, and Don John went up to Claudio and said, "Sir Benedick, I believe?" "The same," lied Claudio.

"I should be much obliged then," said Don John, "if you would use your influence with my brother to cure him of his love for Hero. She is beneath him in rank."

"How do you know he loves her?" inquired

Claudio.

"I heard him swear his affection," was the reply, and Borachio chimed in with, "So did I."

Claudio was then left to himself, and his thought was that his Prince had betrayed him. "Farewell, Hero," he muttered, "I was a fool to trust to an agent."

Meanwhile Beatrice and Benedick (who was masked) were having a brisk exchange of opinions.

"Did Benedick ever make you laugh?" asked she.

"Who is Benedick?" he inquired.

"A Prince's jester," replied Beatrice, and she spoke so sharply that "I would not marry her," he declared afterwards, "if her estate were the Garden of Eden."

But the principal speaker at the masquerade was neither Beatrice nor Benedick. It was Don Pedro, who carried out his plan to the letter, and brought the light back to Claudio's face in a twinkling, by appearing before him with Leonato and Hero, and saying, "Claudio, when would you like to go to church?"

"Tomorrow," was the prompt answer. "Time goes on crutches till I marry Hero."

"Give her a week, my dear son," said Leonato,

and Claudio's heart thumped with joy.

"And now," said the amiable Don Pedro, "we must find a wife for Sir Benedick. It is a task for Hercules."

"I will help you," said Leonato, "if I have to sit up ten nights."

Then Hero spoke. "I will do what I can, my lord, to find a good husband for Beatrice."

Thus, with happy laughter, ended the masquerade which had given Claudio a lesson for nothing.

Borachio cheered up Don John by laying a plan before him with which he was confident he could persuade both Claudio and Don Pedro that Hero was a fickle girl who had two strings to her bow. Don John agreed to this plan of hate.

Don Pedro, on the other hand, had devised a cunning plan of love. "If," he said to Leonato, "we pretend, when Beatrice is near enough to overhear us, that Benedick is pining for her love, she will pity him, see his good qualities, and love him. And if, when Benedick thinks we don't know he is listening, we say how sad it is that the beautiful Beatrice should be in love with a heartless scoffer like Benedick, he will certainly be on his knees before her in a week or less."

So one day, when Benedick was reading in a summerhouse, Claudio sat down outside it with Leonato, and said, "Your daughter told me something about a letter she wrote."

"Letter!" exclaimed Leonato. "She will get up twenty times in the night and write goodness knows what. But once Hero peeped, and saw the words 'Benedick and Beatrice' on the sheet, and then Beatrice tore it up."

"Hero told me," said Claudio, "that she cried, 'O sweet Benedick!'"

Benedick was touched to the core by this improbable story, which he was vain enough to believe. "She is fair and good," he said to himself. "I must not seem proud. I feel that I love her. People will laugh, of course; but their paper bullets will do me no harm."

At this moment Beatrice came to the summerhouse, and said, "Against my will, I have come to tell you that dinner is ready."

"Fair Beatrice, I thank you," said Benedick.

"I took no more pains to come than you take pains to thank me," was the answer, intended to freeze him.

But it did not freeze him. It warmed him. The meaning he squeezed out of her rude speech was that she was delighted to come to him.

Hero, who had undertaken the task of melting the heart of Beatrice, took no trouble to seek an occasion. She simply said to her maid Margaret one day, "Run into the parlor and whisper to Beatrice that Ursula and I are talking about her in the orchard."

Having said this, she felt as sure that Beatrice would overhear what was meant for her ears as if she had made an appointment with her cousin.

In the orchard was a bower, screened from the sun by honeysuckles, and Beatrice entered it a few minutes after Margaret had gone on her errand.

"But are you sure," asked Ursula, who was one of Hero's attendants, "that Benedick loves Beatrice so devotedly?"

"So say the Prince and my Claudio," replied Hero, "and they wished me to tell her, but I said,

'No! Let Benedick get over it.'"

"Why did you say that?"

"Because Beatrice is unbearably proud. Her eyes sparkle with disdain and scorn. She is too conceited to love. I should not like to see her making game of poor Benedick's love. I would rather see Benedick waste away like a covered fire."

"I don't agree with you," said Ursula. "I think your cousin is too clear-sighted not to see the merits of Benedick."

"He is the one man in Italy, except Claudio," said Hero.

The talkers then left the orchard, and Beatrice, excited and tender, stepped out of the summerhouse, saying to herself, "Poor dear Benedick, be true to me, and your love shall tame this wild heart of mine."

We now return to the plan of hate.

The night before the day fixed for Claudio's wedding, Don John entered a room in which Don Pedro and Claudio were conversing, and asked Claudio if he intended to be married tomorrow.

"You know he does!" said Don Pedro.

"He may know differently," said Don John, "when he has seen what I will show him if he will follow me."

They followed him into the garden; and they saw a lady leaning out of Hero's window talking love to Borachio.

Claudio thought the lady was Hero, and said, "I will shame her for it tomorrow!" Don Pedro thought she was Hero, too; but she was not Hero; she was Margaret.

Don John chuckled noiselessly when Claudio and Don Pedro quitted the garden; he gave Borachio a purse containing a thousand ducats.

The money made Borachio feel very gay, and when he was walking in the street with his friend Conrade, he boasted of his wealth and the giver, and told what he had done.

A watchman overheard them, and thought that a man who had been paid a thousand ducats for bad deeds was worth taking in charge. He therefore arrested Borachio and Conrade, who spent the rest of the night in prison.

Before noon of the next day half the aristocrats in Messina were at church. Hero thought it was her wedding day, and she was there in her wedding dress, no cloud on her pretty face or in her frank and shining eyes.

The priest was Friar Francis.

Turning to Claudio, he said, "You come here, my lord, to marry this lady?" "No!" objected Claudio.

Leonato thought he was quibbling over grammar. "You should have said, Friar," said he, "'you come to be married to her.'"

Friar Francis turned to Hero. "Lady," he said, "you come here to be married to this Count?" "I do," replied Hero.

"If either of you know any impediment to this marriage, I charge you to utter it," said the Friar.

"Do you know of any, Hero?" asked Claudio. "None," said she.

"Do you know of any, Count?" demanded the Friar. "I dare reply for him, 'None,'" said Leonato.

Claudio exclaimed bitterly, "O! What will not men dare say! Father," he continued, "will you give me your daughter?" "As freely," replied Leonato, "as God gave her to me."

"And what can I give you," asked Claudio, "which is worthy of this gift?" "Nothing," said Don Pedro, "unless you give the gift back to the giver."

"Sweet Prince, you teach me," said Claudio. "There, Leonato, take her back."

These brutal words were followed by others which flew from Claudio, Don Pedro and Don John.

The church seemed no longer sacred. Hero took her own part as long as she could, then she fainted. All her persecutors left the church, except her father, who was befooled by the accusations against her, and cried, "Let her die!"

But Friar Francis saw Hero blameless with his clear eyes that probed the soul. "She is innocent," he said, "a thousand signs have told me so."

Hero revived under his kind gaze. Her father, flurried and angry, knew not what to think, and the Friar said, "They have left her as one dead with shame. Let us pretend that she is dead until the truth is declared, and slander turns to remorse."

"The Friar advises well," said Benedick. Then Hero was led away into a retreat, and Beatrice and Benedick remained alone in the church.

Benedick knew Beatrice had been weeping bitterly and long. "Surely I do believe your fair cousin is wronged," he said. She still wept.

"Is it not strange," asked Benedick, gently, "that I love nothing in the world as well as you?"

"It were as possible for me to say I loved nothing as well as you," said Beatrice, "but I do not say it. I am sorry for my cousin."

"Tell me what to do for her," said Benedick. "Kill Claudio," said Beatrice.

"Ha! not for the wide world," said Benedick. "Your refusal kills me," said Beatrice. "Farewell."

"Enough! I will challenge him," cried Benedick.

During this scene Borachio and Conrade were in prison. There they were examined by a constable called Dogberry.

The watchman gave evidence to the effect that Borachio had said that he had received a thousand ducats for conspiring against Hero.

Leonato was not present at this examination, but he was nevertheless now thoroughly convinced of Hero's innocence. He played the part of bereaved father very well, and when Don Pedro and Claudio called on him in a friendly way, he said to the Italian, "You have slandered my child to death, and I challenge you to combat."

"I cannot fight an old man," said Claudio.

"You could kill a girl," sneered Leonato, and Claudio's face turned red.

Hot words grew from hot words, and both Don Pedro and Claudio were feeling scorched when Leonato left the room and Benedick entered.

"The old man," said Claudio, "was like to have snapped my nose off."

"You are a villain!" said Benedick, shortly. "Fight me when and with what weapon you please, or I call you a coward."

Claudio was astounded, but said, "I'll meet you. Nobody shall say I can't carve a calf's head."

Benedick smiled, and as it was time for Don Pedro to receive officials, the Prince sat down in a chair of state and prepared his mind for justice.

The door soon opened to admit Dogberry and his prisoners.

"What offence," said Don Pedro, "are these men charged with?"

Borachio laid the whole blame on Don John, who had disappeared. "The lady Hero being dead," he said, "I desire nothing but the reward of a murderer."

Claudio heard with anguish and deep repentance.

Upon the reentrance of Leonato be said to him, "This slave makes clear your daughter's innocence. Choose your revenge."

"Leonato," said Don Pedro, humbly, "I am ready for any penance you may impose."

"I ask you both, then," said Leonato, "to proclaim my daughter's innocence, and to honor her tomb by singing her praise before it. As for you, Claudio, I have this to say: my brother has a daughter so like Hero that she might be a copy of her. Marry her, and my vengeful feelings die."

"Noble sir," said Claudio, "I am yours." Claudio then went to his room and composed a solemn song. Going to the church with Don Pedro and his attendants, he sang it before the monument of Leonato's family. When he had ended he said, "Good night, Hero. Yearly will I do this."

He then gravely, as became a gentleman whose heart was Hero's, made ready to marry a girl whom he did not love. He was told to meet her in Leonato's house, and was faithful to his appointment.

He was shown into a room where Antonio (Leonato's brother) and several masked ladies entered after him. Friar Francis, Leonato, and Benedick were present.

Antonio led one of the ladies towards Claudio.

"Sweet," said the young man, "let me see your face."

"Swear first to marry her," said Leonato.

"Give me your hand," said Claudio to the lady, "before this holy Friar I swear to marry you if you will be my wife."

"Alive I was your wife," said the lady, as she drew off her mask.

"Another Hero!" exclaimed Claudio.

"Hero died," explained Leonato, "only while slander lived."

The Friar was then going to marry the reconciled pair, but Benedick interrupted him with, "Softly, Friar; which of these ladies is Beatrice?"

Here Beatrice unmasked, and Benedick said, "You love me, don't you?"

"Only moderately," was the reply. "Do you love me?"

"Moderately," answered Benedick.

"I was told you were so devoted to me," remarked Beatrice.

"Of you I was told the same," said Benedick.

"Here's your own hand in evidence of your love," said Claudio, producing a feeble sonnet which Benedick had written to his sweetheart. "And here," said Hero, "is a tribute to Benedick, which I picked out of the pocket of Beatrice."

"A miracle!" exclaimed Benedick. "Our hands are against our hearts! Come, I will marry you, Beatrice."

"You shall be my husband to save your life," was the rejoinder.

Benedick kissed her on the mouth; and the Friar married them after he had married Claudio and Hero.

"How is Benedick the married man?" asked Don Pedro.

"Too happy to be made unhappy," replied Benedick. "Crack what jokes you will. As for you, Claudio, I had hoped to fight you, but as you are now my kinsman, live whole and love my cousin."

"My club was in love with you, Benedick, until today," said Claudio; but, "Come, come, let's dance," said Benedick.

And dance they did. Not even the news of the capture of Don John was able to stop the flying feet of the happy lovers, for revenge is not sweet against an evil man who has failed to do harm.

THE TEMPEST

Prospero, the Duke of Milan, was a learned and studious man, who lived among his books, leaving the management of his dukedom to his brother Antonio, in whom indeed he had complete trust. But that trust was ill-rewarded, for Antonio wanted to wear the duke's crown himself, and, to gain his ends, would have killed his brother but for the love the people bore him. However, with the help of Prospero's great enemy, Alonso, King of Naples, he managed to get into his hands the dukedom with all its honor, power, and riches. For they took Prospero to sea, and when they were far away from land, forced him into a little boat with no tackle, mast, or sail. In their cruelty and hatred they put his little daughter, Miranda (not yet three years old), into the boat with him, and sailed away, leaving them to their fate.

But one among the courtiers with Antonio was true to his rightful master, Prospero. To save the duke from his enemies was impossible, but much could be done to remind him of a subject's love. So this worthy lord, whose name was Gonzalo, secretly placed in the boat some fresh water, food, and clothes, and what Prospero valued most of all, some of his precious books.

The boat was cast on an island, and Prospero and his little one landed in safety. Now this island was enchanted, and for years had been under the spell of a wicked witch, Sycorax, who had imprisoned in the trunks of trees all the good spirits she found there. She died shortly before Prospero was cast on those shores, but the spirits, of whom Ariel was the chief, still remained in their prisons.

Prospero was a great magician, for he had devoted himself almost entirely to the study of magic during the years in which he allowed his brother to manage the affairs of Milan. By his art he set free the imprisoned spirits, yet kept them obedient to his will, and they were more truly his subjects than his people in Milan had been. For he treated them kindly as long as they did his bidding, and he exercised his power over them wisely and well. One creature alone he found it necessary to treat with harshness: this was Caliban, the son of the wicked old witch, a hideous, deformed monster, horrible to look on, and vicious and brutal in all his habits.

When Miranda was grown up into a maiden, sweet and fair to see, it chanced that Antonio and Alonso, with Sebastian, his brother, and Ferdinand, his son, were at sea together with old Gonzalo, and their ship came near Prospero's island. Prospero, knowing they were there, raised by his art a great storm, so that even the sailors on board gave themselves up for lost; and first among them all Prince Ferdinand leaped into the sea, and, as his father thought in his grief, was drowned. But Ariel brought him safe ashore; and all the rest of the crew, although they were washed overboard, were landed unhurt in different parts of the island, and the good ship herself, which they all thought had been wrecked, lay at anchor in the harbor whither Ariel had brought her. Such wonders could Prospero and his spirits perform.

While yet the tempest was raging, Prospero showed his daughter the brave ship laboring in the trough of the sea, and told her that it was filled with living human beings like themselves. She, in pity of their lives, prayed him who had raised this storm to quell it. Then her father bade her to have no fear, for he intended to save every one of them.

Then, for the first time, he told her the story of his life and hers, and that he had caused this storm to rise in order that his enemies, Antonio and Alonso, who were on board, might be delivered into his hands.

When he had made an end of his story he charmed her into sleep, for Ariel was at hand, and he had work for him to do. Ariel, who longed for his complete freedom, grumbled to be kept in drudgery, but on being threateningly reminded of all the sufferings he had undergone when Sycorax ruled in the land,

and of the debt of gratitude he owed to the master who had made those sufferings to end, he ceased to complain, and promised faithfully to do whatever Prospero might command.

"Do so," said Prospero, "and in two days I will discharge you."

Then he bade Ariel take the form of a water nymph and sent him in search of the young Prince. And Ariel, invisible to Ferdinand, hovered near him, singing.

And Ferdinand followed the magic singing, as the song changed to a solemn air, and the words brought grief to his heart, and tears to his eyes.

And so singing, Ariel led the spell-bound Prince into the presence of Prospero and Miranda. Then, look! All happened as Prospero desired. For Miranda, who had never, since she could first remember, seen any human being save her father, looked on the youthful Prince with reverence in her eyes, and love in her secret heart.

"I might call him," she said, "a thing divine, for nothing natural I ever saw so noble!"

And Ferdinand, seeing her beauty with wonder and delight, exclaimed—

"Most sure the goddess on whom these airs attend!"

Nor did he attempt to hide the passion which she inspired in him, for scarcely had they exchanged half a dozen sentences, before he vowed to make her his queen if she were willing. But Prospero, though secretly delighted, pretended wrath.

"You come here as a spy," he said to Ferdinand. "I will tie your neck and feet together, and you shall feed on fresh water mussels, withered roots and husk, and have sea-water to drink. Follow."

"No," said Ferdinand, and drew his sword. But on the instant Prospero charmed him so that he stood there like a statue, still as stone; and Miranda in terror prayed her father to have mercy on her lover. But he harshly refused her, and made Ferdinand follow him to his cell. There he set the Prince to work, making him remove thousands of heavy logs of timber and pile them up; and Ferdinand patiently obeyed, and thought his toil all too well repaid by the sympathy of the sweet Miranda.

She in very pity would have helped him in his hard work, but he would not let her, yet he could not keep from her the secret of his love, and she, hearing it, rejoiced and promised to be his wife.

Then Prospero released him from his servitude, and glad at heart, he gave his consent to their marriage.

"Take her," he said, "she is your own."

In the meantime, Antonio and Sebastian in another part of the island were plotting the murder of Alonso, the King of Naples, for Ferdinand being dead, as they thought, Sebastian would succeed to the throne on Alonso's death. And they would have carried out their wicked purpose while their victim was asleep, but that Ariel woke him in good time.

Many tricks did Ariel play them. Once he set a banquet before them, and just as they were going to enjoy it, he appeared to them amid thunder and lightning in the form of a harpy, and immediately the banquet disappeared. Then Ariel scolded them for their sins and vanished too.

Prospero by his enchantments drew them all to the grove, where they waited, trembling and afraid, and now at last bitterly repenting them of their sins.

Prospero determined to make one last use of his magic power, "And then," said he, "I'll break my staff and drown my book."

So he made heavenly music to sound in the air, and appeared to them in his proper shape as the Duke of Milan. Because they repented, he forgave them and told them the story of his life since they had cruelly committed him and his baby daughter to the mercy of wind and waves. Alonso, who seemed sorriest of them all for his past crimes, lamented the loss of his heir. But Prospero drew back a curtain and showed them Ferdinand and Miranda playing at chess. Great was Alonso's joy to greet his loved son again, and when he heard that the fair maid with whom Ferdinand was playing was Prospero's daughter, and that the young folks had been engaged, he said—

"Give me your hands, let grief and sorrow still embrace his heart that does not wish you joy."

So all ended happily. The ship was safe in the

harbor, and next day they all set sail for Naples, where Ferdinand and Miranda were to be married. Ariel gave them calm seas and auspicious gales.

Then Prospero, after many years of absence, went back to his own dukedom, where he was welcomed with great joy by his faithful subjects. He practiced the art of magic no more, but his life was happy, and not only because he had found his own again, but chiefly because, when his bitterest foes who had done him deadly wrong lay at his mercy, he took no revenge on them, but nobly forgave them.

As for Ariel, Prospero made him free as air, so that he could wander where he would, and sing with a light heart his sweet song.

THE WINTER'S TALE

Leontes was the King of Sicily, and his dearest friend was Polixenes, King of Bohemia. They had been brought up together, and only separated when they each had to go and rule over his kingdom. After many years, when each was married and had a son, Polixenes came to stay with Leontes in Sicily.

Leontes was a violent-tempered man and rather silly, and he took it into his stupid head that his wife, Hermione, liked Polixenes better than she did him, her own husband. Once he had got this into his head, nothing could put it out; and he ordered one of his lords, Camillo, to put a poison in Polixenes' wine. Camillo tried to dissuade him from this wicked action, but finding he was not to be moved, pretended to consent. He then told Polixenes what was proposed against him, and they fled from the Court of Sicily that night, and returned to Bohemia, where Camillo lived on as Polixenes' friend and counselor.

Leontes threw the Queen into prison; and her son, the heir to the throne, died of sorrow to see his mother so unjustly and cruelly treated.

While the Queen was in prison she had a little baby, and a friend of hers, named Paulina, had the baby dressed in its best, and took it to show the King, thinking that the sight of his helpless little daughter would soften his heart towards his dear Queen, who had never done him any wrong, and who loved him a great deal more than he deserved; but the King would not look at the baby, and ordered Paulina's husband to take it away in a ship, and leave it in the most desert and dreadful place he could find, which Paulina's husband, very much against his will, was obliged to do.

Then the poor Queen was brought up to be

tried for treason in preferring Polixenes to her King; but really she had never thought of anyone except Leontes, her husband. Leontes had sent some messengers to ask the god, Apollo, whether he was not right in his cruel thoughts of the Queen. But he had no patience to wait till they came back, and so it happened that they arrived in the middle of the trial. The Oracle said—

"Hermione is innocent, Polixenes blameless, Camillo a true subject, Leontes a jealous tyrant, and the King shall live without an heir, if that which is lost be not found."

Then a man came and told them that the little Prince was dead. The poor Queen, hearing this, fell down in a fit; and then the King saw how wicked and wrong he had been. He ordered Paulina and the ladies who were with the Queen to take her away, and try to restore her. But Paulina came back in a few moments, and told the King that Hermione was dead.

Now Leontes' eyes were at last opened to his folly. His Queen was dead, and the little daughter who might have been a comfort to him he had sent away to be the prey of wolves and kites. Life had nothing left for him now. He gave himself up to his grief, and passed many sad years in prayer and remorse.

The baby Princess was left on the seacoast of Bohemia, the very kingdom where Polixenes reigned. Paulina's husband never went home to tell Leontes where he had left the baby; for as he was going back to the ship, he met a bear and was torn to pieces. So there was an end of him.

But the poor deserted little baby was found by a shepherd. She was richly dressed, and had with her some jewels, and a paper was pinned to her cloak, saying that her name was Perdita, and that she came of noble parents.

The shepherd, being a kind-hearted man, took home the little baby to his wife, and they brought it up as their own child. She had no more teaching than a shepherd's child generally has, but she inherited from her royal mother many graces and charms, so that she was quite different from the other maidens in the village where she lived.

One day Prince Florizel, the son of the good King of Bohemia, was hunting near the shepherd's house and saw Perdita, now grown up to a charming woman. He made friends with the shepherd, not telling him that he was the Prince, but saying that his name was Doricles, and that he was a private gentleman; and then, being deeply in love with the pretty Perdita, he came almost daily to see her.

The King could not understand what it was that took his son nearly every day from home; so he set people to watch him, and then found out that the heir of the King of Bohemia was in love with Perdita, the pretty shepherd girl. Polixenes, wishing to see whether this was true, disguised himself, and went with the faithful Camillo, in disguise too, to the old shepherd's house. They arrived at the feast of sheep-shearing, and, though strangers, they were made very welcome. There was dancing going on, and a peddler was selling ribbons and laces and gloves, which the young men bought for their sweethearts.

Florizel and Perdita, however, were taking no

part in this gay scene, but sat quietly together talking. The King noticed the charming manners and great beauty of Perdita, never guessing that she was the daughter of his old friend, Leontes. He said to Camillo—

"This is the prettiest low-born girl that ever ran on the green meadow. Nothing she does or seems but smacks of something greater than herself—too noble for this place."

And Camillo answered, "In truth she is the Queen of this place."

But when Florizel, who did not recognize his father, called upon the strangers to witness his engagement with the pretty shepherdess, the King made himself known and forbade the marriage, adding that if ever she saw Florizel again, he would kill her and her old father, the shepherd; and with that he left them. But Camillo remained behind, for he was charmed with Perdita, and wished to befriend her.

Camillo had long known how sorry Leontes was for that foolish madness of his, and he longed to go back to Sicily to see his old master. He now proposed that the young people should go there and claim the protection of Leontes. So they went, and the shepherd went with them, taking Perdita's jewels, her baby clothes, and the paper he had found pinned to her cloak.

Leontes received them with great kindness. He was very polite to Prince Florizel, but all his looks were for Perdita. He saw how much she was like the Queen Hermione, and said again and again—

"Such a sweet creature my daughter might have been, if I had not cruelly sent her from me."

When the old shepherd heard that the King had lost a baby daughter, who had been left upon the coast of Bohemia, he felt sure that Perdita, the child he had reared, must be the King's daughter, and when he told his tale and showed the jewels and the paper, the King perceived that Perdita was indeed his long-lost child. He welcomed her with joy, and rewarded the good shepherd.

Polixenes had hastened after his son to prevent his marriage with Perdita, but when he found that she was the daughter of his old friend, he was only too glad to give his consent.

Yet Leontes could not be happy. He remembered how his fair Queen, who should have been at his side to share his joy in his daughter's happiness, was dead through his unkindness, and he could say nothing for a long time but—

"Oh, your mother! Your mother!" and asked forgiveness of the King of Bohemia, and then kissed his daughter again, and then the Prince Florizel, and then thanked the old shepherd for all his goodness.

Then Paulina, who had been high all these years in the King's favor, because of her kindness to the dead Queen Hermione, said—"I have a statue made in the likeness of the dead Queen, a piece many years in doing, and performed by the rare Italian master, Giulio Romano. I keep it in a private house apart, and there, ever since you lost your Queen, I have gone twice or thrice a day. Will it please your Majesty to go and see the statue?"

So Leontes and Polixenes, and Florizel and Perdita, with Camillo and their attendants, went to Paulina's house where there was a heavy purple curtain screening off an alcove; and Paulina, with her hand on the curtain, said—

"She was peerless when she was alive, and I do believe that her dead likeness excels whatever yet you have looked upon, or that the hand of man has done. Therefore I keep it lonely, apart. But here it is—look, and say, it is well."

And with that she drew back the curtain and showed them the statue. The King gazed and gazed on the beautiful statue of his dead wife, but said nothing.

"I like your silence," said Paulina, "it shows your wonder. But speak, is it not like her?"

"It is almost herself," said the King, "and yet, Paulina, Hermione was not so much wrinkled, nothing so old as this seems."

"Oh, not by much," said Polixenes.

"Al," said Paulina, "that is the cleverness of the carver, who shows her to us as she would have been had she lived till now."

And still Leontes looked at the statue and could not take his eyes away.

"If I had known," said Paulina, "that this poor image would so have stirred your grief, and love, I would not have shown it to you."

But he only answered, "Do not draw the curtain."

"No, you must not look any longer," said Paulina, "or you will think it moves."

"Let be! let be!" said the King. "Would you not think it breathed?"

"I will draw the curtain," said Paulina, "or you will think it lives presently."

"Ah, sweet Paulina," said Leontes, "make me to think so twenty years together."

"If you can bear it," said Paulina, "I can make the statue move, make it come down and take you by the hand. Only you would think it was by wicked magic."

"Whatever you can make her do, I am content to look on," said the King.

And then, all folks there admiring and watching, the statue moved from its pedestal, and came down the steps and put its arms round the King's neck, and he held her face and kissed her many times, for this was no statue, but the real living Queen Hermione herself. She had lived hidden, by Paulina's kindness, all these years, and would not discover herself to her husband, though she knew he had repented, because she could not quite forgive him till she knew what had become of her little baby.

Now that Perdita was found, she forgave her husband everything, and it was like a new and beautiful marriage to them, to be together once more.

Florizel and Perdita were married and lived long and happily.

To Leontes his many years of suffering were well paid for in the moment when, after long grief and pain, he felt the arms of his true love around him once again.

ALL'S WELL THAT
ENDS WELL

In the year thirteen hundred and something, the Countess of Rousillon was unhappy in her palace near the Pyrenees. She had lost her husband, and the King of France had summoned her son Bertram to Paris, hundreds of miles away.

Bertram was a pretty youth with curling hair, finely arched eyebrows, and eyes as keen as a hawk's. He was as proud as ignorance could make him, and would lie to gain a selfish end. But a pretty youth is a pretty youth, and Helena was in love with him.

Helena was the daughter of a great doctor who had died in the service of the Count of Rousillon.

Her sole fortune consisted in a few of her father's prescriptions.

When Bertram had gone, Helena's sad look was noticed by the Countess, who told her that she was exactly the same to her as her own child. Tears then gathered in Helena's eyes, for she felt that the Countess made Bertram seem like a brother whom she could never marry. The Countess guessed her secret immediately, and Helena confessed that Bertram was to her as the sun is to the day.

She hoped, however, to win this sun by earning the gratitude of the King of France, who suffered from a lingering illness, which made him lame. The great doctors attached to the Court despaired of curing him, but Helena had confidence in a prescription which her father had used with success.

Taking an affectionate leave of the Countess, she went to Paris, and was allowed to see the King.

He was very polite, but it was plain he thought her a quack. "It would not become me," he said, "to apply to a simple maiden for the relief which all the learned doctors cannot give me."

"Heaven uses weak instruments sometimes," said Helena, and she declared that she would be put to death if she failed to make him well.

"And if you succeed?" questioned the King.

"Then I will ask your Majesty to give me for a husband the man whom I choose!"

So earnest a young lady could not be resisted forever by a suffering king. Helena, therefore, became the King's doctor, and in two days the royal cripple could skip.

He summoned his courtiers, and they made a glittering crowd in his palace. Well might the country girl have been dazzled, and seen a dozen husbands worth dreaming of among the handsome young noblemen before her. But her eyes only wandered till they found Bertram. Then she went up to him, and said, "I dare not say I take you, but I am yours!" Raising her voice that the King might hear, she added, "This is the Man!"

"Bertram," said the King, "take her; she's your wife!"

"My wife?" said Bertram. "I beg your Majesty to

permit me to choose a wife."

"Do you know, Bertram, what she has done for your King?" asked the monarch, who had treated Bertram like a son.

"Yes, your Majesty," replied Bertram, "but why should I marry a girl who owes her breeding to my father's charity?"

"You disdain her for lacking a title, but I can give her a title," said the King; and as he looked at the sulky youth a thought came to him, and he added, "Strange that you think so much of blood when you could not distinguish your own from a beggar's if you saw them mixed together in a bowl."

"I cannot love her," asked Bertram; and Helena said gently, "Urge him not, your Majesty. I am glad to have cured my King for my country's sake."

"My honor requires that boy's obedience," said the King. "Bertram, make up your mind to this. You marry this lady, of whom you are so unworthy, or you learn how a king can hate. Your answer?"

Bertram bowed low and said, "Your Majesty has ennobled the lady. I submit."

"Take her by the hand," said the King, "and tell her she is yours."

Bertram obeyed, and with little delay he was married to Helena.

Fear of the King, however, could not make him a lover. Ridicule helped to sour him. A base soldier named Parolles told him to his face that now he had a "kicky-wicky" his business was not to fight but to stay at home. Bertram felt he could not bear having a wife, and that he must go to the war in Italy, though the King had forbidden him.

He ordered Helena to take leave of the King and return to Rousillon, giving her letters for his mother and herself. He then rode off, bidding her a cold goodbye.

She opened the letter addressed to herself, and read, "When you can get the ring from my finger you can call me husband, but I bet you can never get it."

Dry-eyed had Helena been when she entered the King's presence and said farewell, but he was uneasy on her account, and gave her a ring from his own finger, saying, "If you send this to me, I shall know you are in trouble, and help you."

She did not show him Bertram's letter to his wife; it would have made him wish to kill the irresponsible Count; but she went back to Rousillon and handed her mother-in-law the second letter. It was short and bitter. "I have run away," it said. "If the world be broad enough, I will be always far away from her."

"Cheer up," said the noble widow to the deserted wife. "I wash his name out of my blood, and you alone are my child."

The Dowager Countess, however, was still mother enough to Bertram to lay the blame of his conduct on Parolles, whom she called "a very bad fellow."

Helena did not stay long at Rousillon. She dressed herself as a pilgrim, and, leaving a letter for her mother-in-law, secretly set out for Florence.

On entering that city she asked a woman the way to the Pilgrims' House of Rest, but the woman begged "the holy pilgrim" to lodge with her.

Helena found that her hostess was a widow, who had a beautiful daughter named Diana.

When Diana heard that Helena came from France, she said, "A countryman of yours, Count Rousillon, has done worthy service for Florence." But after a time, Diana had something to tell which was not at all worthy of Helena's husband. Bertram was making love to Diana. He did not hide the fact that he was married, but Diana heard from Parolles that his wife was not worth caring for.

The widow was anxious for Diana's sake, and Helena decided to inform her that she was the Countess Rousillon.

"He keeps asking Diana for a lock of her hair," said the widow.

Helena smiled mournfully, for her hair was as fine as Diana's and of the same color. Then an idea struck her, and she said, "Take this purse of gold for yourself. I will give Diana three thousand crowns if she will help me to carry out this plan. Let her promise to give a lock of her hair to my husband if he will give her the ring which he wears on his finger. It is an ancestral ring. Five Counts of Rousillon have worn it, yet he will yield it up for a lock of your daughter's hair. Let your daughter insist that he shall cut the lock of hair from her in a dark room, and agree in advance that she shall not speak a single word."

The widow listened attentively, with the purse of gold in her lap. She said at last, "I consent, if Diana is willing."

Diana was willing, and, strange to say, the prospect of cutting off a lock of hair from a silent girl in a dark room was so pleasing to Bertram that he handed Diana his ring, and was told when to follow her into the dark room. At the time appointed he came with a sharp knife, and felt a sweet face touch his as he cut off the lock of hair, and he left the room satisfied, and on his finger was a ring which the girl in the dark room had given him.

The war was nearly over, but one of its concluding chapters taught Bertram that the soldier who had called Helena his "kicky-wicky" was far less courageous than a wife. Parolles was such a boaster, and so fond of trimings to his clothes, that the French officers played him a trick to discover what he was made of. He had lost his drum, and had said that he would regain it unless he was killed in the battle. He failed, and he was inventing the story of a heroic failure, when he was surrounded and disarmed.

"Portotartarossa," said a French lord.

"What does this mean?" thought Parolles, whose eyes had been covered.

"He's calling for the tortures," said a French man, pretending to act as interpreter. "What will you say to avoid them?"

"As much," replied Parolles, "as I could possibly say if you beat me hard." He was as good as his word. He told them how many there were in each regiment of the Florentine army, and he refreshed them with anecdotes of the officers commanding it.

Bertram was present, and heard a letter read, in which Parolles told Diana that he was a fool.

"This is your devoted friend," said a French lord.

"He is a cat to me now," said Bertram, who detested our hearthrug pets.

Parolles was finally let go, but from then on he felt like a sneak, and was not addicted to boasting.

We now return to France with Helena, who had

spread a report of her death, which was conveyed to the Dowager Countess at Rousillon by Lafeu, a lord who wished to marry his daughter Magdalen to Bertram.

The King mourned for Helena, but he approved of the marriage proposed for Bertram, and paid a visit to Rousillon in order to see it accomplished.

"His great offense is dead," he said. "Let Bertram approach me."

Then Bertram, scarred in the cheek, knelt before his Sovereign, and said that if he had not loved Lafeu's daughter before he married Helena, he would have cherished his wife, whom he now loved when it was too late.

"Love that is late offends the Great Sender," said the King. "Forget sweet Helena, and give a ring to Magdalen."

Bertram immediately gave a ring to Lafeu, who said angrily, "It's Helena's!"

"It's not!" said Bertram.

The King looked at the ring, and said, "This is the ring I gave to Helena, and asked her to send to me if ever she needed help. So you cheated to get from her what could help her most."

Bertram denied again that the ring was Helena's, but even his mother said it was.

"You lie!" exclaimed the King. "Seize him, guards!" but even while they were seizing him, Bertram wondered how the ring, which he thought Diana had given him, came to be so like Helena's. A gentleman now entered, giving a letter to the King. It was signed Diana Capilet, and it begged that the King would order Bertram to marry her whom he had deserted after winning her love.

"I'd rather buy a son-in-law at a fair than take Bertram now," said Lafeu.

"Let Diana in," said the King.

Bertram found himself confronted by Diana and her mother. He denied that Diana had any relationship with him, and spoke of her as though her life was spent in the gutter. But she asked him why he had given a girl, the ring of his ancestors which now was missing from his finger.

Bertram was ready to sink into the earth, but fate

was most generous to him. Helena entered.

"Do I see reality?" asked the King.

"O pardon! pardon!" cried Bertram.

She held up his ancestral ring. "Now that I have this," said she, "will you love me, Bertram?"

"To the end of my life," cried he.

"My eyes smell onions," said Lafeu. Tears for Helena were twinkling in them.

The King praised Diana when he was fully informed by that not very shy young lady of the meaning of her conduct. For Helena's sake she had wished to expose Bertram's meanness, not only to the King, but to himself. His pride was now in shreds, and it is believed that he made a husband of some sort after all.

有声双语经典

图书在版编目（CIP）数据

莎士比亚喜剧故事／（英）威廉·莎士比亚（William Shakespeare）著；
（英）伊迪丝·内斯比特（Edith Nesbit）改写；黄晓丽译 . —南京：译林出
版社，2022.2
（有声双语经典）
ISBN 978-7-5447-8959-2

Ⅰ.①莎… Ⅱ.①威…②伊…③黄… Ⅲ.①英语－汉语－对照读物
②喜剧－剧本－作品集－英国－中世纪 Ⅳ.①H319.4：I

中国版本图书馆 CIP 数据核字（2021）第 237777 号

莎士比亚喜剧故事　[英国] 威廉·莎士比亚／著　[英国] 伊迪丝·内斯比特／改写
　　　　　　　　　黄晓丽／译

责任编辑　许　昆
装帧设计　侯海屏
校　　对　孙玉兰
责任印制　董　虎

出版发行　译林出版社
地　　址　南京市湖南路 1 号 A 楼
邮　　箱　yilin@yilin.com
网　　址　www.yilin.com
市场热线　025-86633278
排　　版　南京展望文化发展有限公司
印　　刷　江苏凤凰新华印务集团有限公司
开　　本　880毫米 ×1240毫米　1/32
印　　张　5.875
插　　页　4
版　　次　2022 年 2 月第 1 版
印　　次　2022 年 2 月第 1 次印刷
书　　号　ISBN 978-7-5447-8959-2
定　　价　32.00 元